RESILIENCE

It's not about bouncing back

How leaders and organizations can build
resilience before disruption hits

Jennifer Eggers & Cynthia Barlow

Enjoy your
resilience journey!
Jennifer Eggs

Published by Best Seller Publishing®, Pasadena, CA
Best Seller Publishing® is a registered trademark
Printed in the United States of America.

ISBN: 978-1-079791-07-5

For more information, please write:
Best Seller Publishing®
1346 Walnut Street, #205
Pasadena, CA 91106
or call 1(626) 765 9750
Toll Free: 1(844) 850-3500
Visit us online at: www.BestSellerPublishing.org

We dedicate this book to:

Our parents, who never doubted,
Our God, who never wavered, and to
the doctors in our lives who made it possible to live.

More praise for Resilience: It's NOT about Bouncing Back

Bouncing back from adversity is not enough. Resilience is about learning, adapting and getting stronger and better. The authors have a formula for continuous improvement and long-term success which every leader should learn and apply. **Resilience: It's Not About Bouncing Back** is a "must-read" [that presents] a unique, teachable framework applicable to individuals and organizations!"

Lance Miyamoto
Chief HR Officer, Catalent

"If you want to build more resilience *intentionally*—personally and professionally—read this book.

Fran Karamousis
Chief of Research, Gartner

"Any of us that choose to tackle life's important challenges know it takes a lot out of us. Good days and tough days. We also deal with what life throws our way by virtue of being human. Resilience is what it takes to *thrive* – not simply survive. Jennifer and Cynthia's thoughtful work helps us to stop, reflect and build this capacity in ourselves and our larger worlds. To paraphrase them, it's not about bouncing back. It's about rising."

Al Preble
Managing Partner, Cambridge Leadership Group

"This book takes complex, academic research and makes it come to life in real and relevant ways. [It offers] a fresh perspective that marries academic research and practical application."

Jeff Prosinski
Chief Financial Officer, JM Huber Corporation

"In my 30-year career leading International businesses and cross functional projects, this book reinforces my belief that resilience and building trust are the common denominators of great teams that deliver big results and individual fulfillment. Any leader will benefit from the study of these concepts."

Halsey M. Cook Jr.
President and CEO Milliken & Company

"A trusted roadmap for the self-conscious leader wanting to evolve their leadership and communications skill. Cynthia and Jennifer provide the perfect synthesis of insights that are both evocatively philosophical and also utterly practical."

John Larsen
EVP & National Practice Lead (Crisis & Risk) Edelman

"If you lead teams, community organizations or businesses, the exceptional personal experience and extraordinary research presented by Jennifer and Cynthia will help you make a positive impact and thrive through change."

Shawn Boom
CEO, Vanco and Ultramarathoner

"**Resilience: It's NOT About Bouncing Back** is a corporate culture transformational game changer! It is a must read for leaders supporting their employees and teams through business disruption. It shows the way to lead authentically & courageously, while staying true to your companies' brand, values and corporate culture to drive lasting transformational change."

Tim Morton,
Founder & Managing Partner, Prompta Consulting Group

This book reaffirms that no matter what challenges we face, there is always an opportunity to level up personally or professionally. This is especially true for those who lead people. The resilience mindset starts from the top. **Resilience: It's NOT About Bouncing Back** needs to be in the hands of every company's executive team yesterday to be poised to thrive for the future.

Julia Cartwright,
Head of People and Culture, GroupBy, Inc

"This book captures the transformational concepts that Cynthia has provided the Valitas team over the last few years. In a business where trust and integrity in the face of high pressure is an absolute requirement, these concepts have made the difference."

Paris Aden, Founder
Valitas Capital Partners

Table of Contents

Introduction xi

Chapter 1: Resilience: What it Is, Isn't, and Why It Is
The Most Critical Skill For Leaders 11

PART 1 – BUILDING INDIVIDUAL RESILIENCE

Chapter 2: The First Step: Understand the Filters You Use 39

Chapter 3: Create A Mindset to Minimize Stress:
Authenticity & Attitude 63

Chapter 4: *Derailers Of a Resilient Mindset:* How Your
Comfort Zone Holds You Hostage
(And How to Break Free) 83

Chapter 5: *Derailers Of a Resilient Mindset:* Guilt and
Resentment: Cancers that Eat Resilience Alive 93

Chapter 6: Intentional Choices: How to Stop Choosing
Without Thinking 107

Chapter 7: Choices that Banish Change Fatigue Forever 121

Chapter 8: Know Your Purpose: The Best Preparation
for Rapid, Disruptive Change 135

Chapter 9:   Define Success: Make the Right Choices
             in the Heat of Stress 145

Chapter 10: Core Beliefs: Know What You Stand on
            When You Need to Stand Up 159

PART 2 – BUILDING RESILIENT TEAMS & ORGANIZATIONS

Chapter 11: Building a Resilient Team 171

Chapter 12: The First Step: Create Alignment 185

Chapter 13: Create a Resilient Team Mindset 207

Chapter 14: How Comfort Zones Hold Organizations
            Hostage (And How to Break Free) 215

Chapter 15: Two Major Derailers to Organizational
            Resilience (And How to Stop Them) 221

Chapter 16: Choices That Drive Resilience and Build Trust.......... 239

Chapter 17: How Your Purpose, Definition of Success
            and Core Beliefs Foster Alignment 245

CONCLUSION

Chapter 18: Where to Go from Here 255

We Can Help 261

Authors Notes & Bio: Jennifer Eggers 263

Authors Notes & Bio: Cynthia Barlow 267

Bibliography & Additional Reading 271

Acknowledgements 273

Introduction

On April 11, 1970, the Apollo 13 spacecraft, Odyssey, lifted off from Cape Canaveral for man's third trip to the moon. It was an exciting moment for NASA, the flight staff and the three astronauts; Jim Lovell, Fred Haise and Jack Swigert. It was also a near rendezvous with death for these brave men.

It began innocently enough. On the evening of April 13, the engineers at Mission Control in Houston observed a low-pressure warning signal on an oxygen tank in Odyssey and instructed Swigert to conduct a routine procedure called a, "cryo stir," designed to stop the super cold gas from settling into layers and eventually causing damage to the craft.

Swigert flipped the switch and all hell broke loose. Alarm lights lit up like the Fourth of July, oxygen pressure plummeted and all power in the spacecraft disappeared. He then radioed one of the most understated phrases in American history, "Houston, we've had a problem."

This was tantamount to a Titanic crew member informing his captain, "We've sort of hit an iceberg." Odyssey was not only in danger of aborting its mission to the moon but of becoming a space coffin for three doomed men.

An investigation later determined that faulty wires had been exposed in the oxygen tank and that had led to an entire side of the ship being devastated. The astronauts were in trouble. The entire world watched with concern as the engineers in Houston and the men in space worked to bring the crippled craft home safely.

The story of how they did it can be summarized in one word: Resilience.

It was the kind of adaptive thinking, ingenuity, creativity and guts that define the word, both for individuals and for organizations. The only way it could have been pulled off successfully was if everyone involved pulled together and, as a powerfully functioning unit, mobilized every resource they had to perform a miracle.

And, they did.

The NASA engineers and astronauts in Houston, along with the three men in space, made several resilient moves that changed Odyssey from a crippled ship to a functioning marvel that landed safely on earth.

✳ ✳ ✳ ✳ ✳

Those NASA folks could have written a compelling book about resilience. In fact, almost *anyone* could write a book about resilience. If you've been hit by a car or truck, lost a loved one, lost a job, or had a serious illness and come out on the other side, you likely know something about what it means to be resilient. There are shelves full of books written about resilience by people who discovered it deep in themselves. While the authors of this book have fallen into that category many times over, this is not a "tell-our-story" kind of book.

Instead, we want to underscore and emphasize the power of resilience within organizations and how it can transform an average company into a powerhouse. Resilience can enable teams to higher, more productive performance levels. Resilience is likely the single most important characteristic of leaders today, but very few people are talking about it, particularly in the organizational context. Even in todays' environment of rapid disruptive change, there is still no manual for how to build resilient organizations. Yet there is a simple framework that can be used by leaders and teams to create it.

That is why Cynthia and I wrote this book.

Jennifer works with leaders and executives that want to create alignment and improve their organization's capacity to adapt. She never set out to lead personal growth work. Cynthia does, though, and is great at it. Over decades of working with leaders in nearly every industry, and through the process of writing this book, **we have also learned that until we do the work required as *people*, we cannot do the work required of us as *leaders*,** and without that, we cannot possibly do the work required as organizations. For that reason, this book is divided into two parts: How to build resilience as an individual, as a leader; and in the second part, how to build more resilient teams and organizations.

When people are broken, businesses and organizations break, too. When people become more resilient, they are better equipped to build organizations resilient enough to innovate, sustain and come back stronger in environments of rapid, disruptive change. Resilience is required in order to navigate the volatile, uncertain, complex and ambiguous (**VUCA**) world in which we live.

Resilience, left merely to individuals, will be built by people only in the moments that require them to dig deep and find it. That's a singular and solitary experience. The real power in building resilience, *really* building it, intentionally and before we need it, lies in what we can accomplish when our organizations become resilient, i.e. when we are resilient *together*. If left only to individuals, we will each become as resilient as we need to be to muddle through and emerge from our own *individual* messes. But, together, we can build organizations that can rebound, grow, and even change the world. We look more closely at this notion in Part Two.

The power for organizations lies in the act of methodically and collaboratively building a *collective* Resilience Framework to increase their ability to thrive in the face of complex challenges for which the answers, and often even the *definition of* the problems themselves, may not be obvious. In many organizations, these challenges come by way of rapid, disruptive change that requires both the organizations and the leaders within them to make tradeoffs in values and loyalties. Often, individuals' resilience will "get them through" such changes. Sometimes. A more effective approach is to drive the focus toward building organizational resilience.

A high tide lifts all boats, they say.

We hope reading this book will lift yours.

Note to the reader*: While this book has been written by two authors, we have made every effort to speak in one voice to avoid the reader having to identify who is speaking. Unless otherwise noted, the pronouns:*

- *I refers to the author*

- *We refers to the reader and the authors (all of us collectively)*

- *You is used primarily in the exercises and in reference directly to the reader*

- *They is used in context*

All quotes are attributed to both of us.

CHAPTER 1

Resilience: What It Is, Isn't, And Why It Is The Most Critical Skill For Leaders

*"Resilience is all about being able to overcome
the unexpected. Sustainability is about survival.
The goal of resilience is to thrive."*

– Jamais Cascio

It was the spring of 2004 and I was test-driving a red 2002 Ford Thunderbird. It was the dream I had wanted since I was old enough to drive. And now, I could finally afford it. I had never felt so free as I sped down the highway on top of the world—until the phone rang.

My boss began to scream at me over the phone. Stunned, I pulled over to the side of the road as he berated me.

He had discovered that I had dared to disagree with his boss. And I had, loudly, in a meeting, in front of others. What he did not know was that I had also gone to his boss's office to clear the air and she and I had come to an understanding. In the end, she respected me for speaking up and I had new-found respect for her (and a new set of assumptions for next time). But the guy in the middle was irate He continued to criticize me for a couple of days, during which my own anger increased. And though he finally gave it up, a week later my anger began to affect our interactions. How could it not?

He finally called me into his office. I'm not sure what I expected, but it wasn't what he said. He looked me in the eye and said, "Jennifer, things happen. You're angry. I'm angry. But if you can't get over it, you will never be able to lead. You need to get back in the game faster when you get knocked down, or you are done."

His words stung. But they were true. The show had to go on, yet how could I ever trust him again?

This dilemma disoriented me enough to change the course of my career. I had to figure out how to rise above all the messy, miserable crap that happens at all levels of leadership. My boss was right. I had to get past it. Was that called resilience? I began to research. There wasn't much there. Perhaps the most common description of resilience I came across was, *"The ability to bounce back from stress, crisis and setbacks."*

But in dealing with my abusive boss, I couldn't seem to bounce at all, let alone bounce *back*. I was stuck, unable to move forward as if a lead balloon had been tied to my foot to hold me there. I knew that if I didn't overcome this, his stinging words would become a millstone around my neck. But I was also pretty sure I could never go "back".

I found a ball to test the bouncing back concept. While bouncing the ball, I realized something significant: After it hit the ground it never came back as high as where it had started. The concept of "bouncing back" was not the answer. That's not enough. Once you bounce a ball, it eventually peters out and stops moving.

Harvard Business Review editor (and one of a few who have written about resilience), Diane Coutu agrees that "anything to do with bouncing back greatly minimizes the struggle and the growth required to build genuine resilience, as well as the adaptations one must make to emerge stronger from a stressful situation." Resilience is not about bouncing back. Resilience is about moving forward more energized, elevated and equipped for what's next.

Building resilience involves intentional preparation to increase the ability to emerge from challenges better equipped to deal with the next. This is not a return to the former state of mind or to the past. It is a transformation into a *stronger* self, so that the next time disruption hits one will be better prepared. For organizations facing rapid, disruptive change, there is often no "back" to bounce to after disruption, because by the time the organization rights itself, things have changed. The most entrepreneurial woman I know, Karla Trotman, CEO and founder of several businesses, observed that "the pace of change in organizations is often so intense that by the time you expend the effort to come back, the organization is, more than likely, far behind."

There is a huge need to build resilience, both for individuals and for organizations. I came to discover that while resilience may be the most critical characteristic for effective leadership, no one was talking about it. We (the authors) decided to change that.

Defining Resilience

In LeaderShift® Insights' Resilience Workshop, we ask people to choose their favorite definition of resilience from the list below:

- The capacity to mobilize personal features that enable [the organization] to prevent, tolerate, overcome and be enhanced by adverse events and experiences (Mowbray, 2010).

- The ability to stay problem-focused, on task and energized when facing challenges, large scale change and ambiguity (Becker, 2014).

- Intelligent deployment of limited resources – not trying to change what we can't control, but also not giving up prematurely and missing opportunities to put our resources where they can maximize impact (Becker, 2014).

- The Serenity prayer:

"God, grant me the serenity to accept the things
I cannot change, courage to change the things
I can and wisdom to know the difference."

I personally like the Serenity Prayer. I use it to get myself back in control and make intentional choices. But truthfully, none of these definitions do justice to the concept of resilience.

For the purpose of this book, I would like to offer this definition:

Resilience is the power to be energized and elevated by
disruption. It is the internal fortitude to emerge stronger
and even more effective from tough situations.

Building resilience involves very intentional preparation. We are building a foundation on which we can rely, before situations get tough, to increase our ability to come back better equipped than we were before.

Resilience Is NOT the Same Thing As Coping

Coping is the ability to get past a difficult situation in the moment. In the moment when we need to cope, it is far too late to build resilience. Resilience is a different beast all together. If we truly build resilience, the need to cope becomes a lot less necessary.

Resilience is built over time. We can build resilience intentionally, but to be energized and elevated by disruption, this preparation must happen before the disruption hits. Coping is about merely surviving or "getting through." It has little to do with being energized or elevated, and even less to do with finding meaning in a situation or preparing for the next. Coping, while sometimes necessary, can be exhausting.

Resilience is not a means to an end. It is another end—an end way beyond coping.

Resilience acknowledges that life is hard and that there will be challenges that will knock us down and prompts us to prepare, not just to fall, but to get back up and rise, stronger and better for it.

If we are leading organizations and teams that must adapt quickly to change, we need resilience for two reasons. First, because we will get knocked down. The nature of work requires us to adapt. Second, sooner or later, as leaders, we will be responsible for this kind of work. At some point, we will need to mobilize people to solve adaptive challenges. These challenges will require raising tough questions that others may not want to answer. We will need to mobilize people to think and act in ways that they may never have done and may not want to. This kind of leadership is not easy. Stepping into that role means not that we might get banged up, but that we *will* get banged up. Adaptive leadership is not always safe, but it is necessary. If we are going to be resilient, we will need to be personally responsible to run *into* the fight, not to merely cope with it. This requires a tremendous amount of preparation.

It has precious little to do with being able to cope.

Can Resilience be Learned?

To build corporate (organizational) resilience, it is very helpful for individuals in the organization (or at least the leaders) to master this skill first. This begs the question: Can resilience be taught? The answer: Absolutely. Not only can resilience be taught, it can be scaled to an organizational level. This book will explain how.

Let's begin with a fact: One does not need to have had trouble personally to become resilient. Stories abound of those inspired by resilient people who have triumphed over tragedies. Research has proven over and over that yes, resilience can be learned. The key to learning how to do so is to *build a framework* that you (or your organization) can fall back on when things get tough, and to build it *intentionally*.

Building a Resilience Framework is personal. It's edgy; it can feel like a sudden burst of cold air in your face. It gets under your skin and asks deep personal questions about how you became the person you are, and how who you are shapes you as a leader. It dares you to delve into who you want to become.

Imagine building the same framework for a team or large company. Becoming resilient requires leadership teams to align around the things that are most critical to driving what (and who) the organization wants to be when the chips are down.

Right before 9/11, I went through the US Marine Corps civilian anti-violence and counter-terror training. I was in a role where I travelled globally, and the company required the training. The idea was that executives would be able to anticipate and plan responses to specific situations *before* they occurred. This allowed for narrow, focused action in the moment because instead of having to think, the plan for what to do was already clear.

Another example of using a Resilience Framework is the story of Todd Staszak.

Todd was fifteen years old, from Hatteras, North Carolina, when he jumped in to action to save a young boy's life in a deadly rip tide. Todd was a body-boarder and before he got involved in his hobby, he used his training as a Boy Scout, following their motto, "Be Prepared."

Staszak prepared for any eventuality in the ocean by learning all he could about the movements and oceanic behaviors of rip tides, learning underwater shoal movements and their hidden perils and how to extricate himself from danger if he ever fell off his board into the volatile sea.

His intentional framework prepared him for the day he heard a young boy screaming for help 150 yards from the shoreline. The tide was pulling the boy under. The boy's father stood helplessly, watching the horrific scene from the shore as his son slowly sank into the ocean.

Todd heard the screams and began paddling his small board to the struggling child. He took hold of him and realized the boy had been trying to swim against the current which caused him to be swept further away from safety. He was gasping for air, within minutes of death.

Todd understood this particular current. He loaded the boy at the point of a large wave which crested toward land and it literally shot the kid all the way to the shore. The grateful father ran into the shallow water and carried his son to the sand where he coughed up water and was soon breathing normally again.

Todd's preparation ahead of time made handling the dangerous situation second nature. It was as though he were on autopilot. Once he saw the youngster was all right, Todd resumed his body boarding and enjoyed his afternoon. Like a good Scout, he had been well prepared months before this emergency took place.

Todd learned a philosophy and received a set of tools before he needed them. He had a toolkit, of sorts, and he knew which tool would solve which type of problem so that when he encountered the problems, he was prepared, too.

Resilience works the same way.

We can build a framework *before* the need arises so that when things get tough, we and the people around us in our organizations shift into autopilot. This is not only smart business; it is corporate brilliance.

Those who have trained in a discipline like Six Sigma, carpentry, or engineering, have seen this at work. We learned how to use a process and a set of tools *before* we needed them. Familiarity with the toolkit equipped us to apply our best thinking when we encountered problems. Leadership, particularly in the face of complex adaptive challenges, doesn't always work that way, but our ability to show up the way we want to is directly proportional to our ability to prepare for it.

As a professional leader, making decisions is non-negotiable. But making *wise* decisions will make or break a project or a company.

Characteristics of Resilience

Diane Coutu has written perhaps the most noted work on resilience. She defines three characteristics for resilient people and organizations. Our work with hundreds of organizations and thousands of people validates her conclusions and supports the notion that they are shared by organizations. This is good news for companies trying to thrive in the face of rapid, disruptive change.

The key is that you need *all* of the following characteristics to become truly resilient. As Coutu said, "You can bounce back from hardship with one or two of these qualities, but you **will only be truly resilient with all three.**"

The three characteristics of resilient people and organizations, paraphrased from Coutu, are:

- A firm grasp on reality (she goes so far as to call this "staunch acceptance")

- A deep belief that what you're doing is meaningful

- The ability to improvise

1.   A firm grasp on **REALITY**

Coutu challenges a common belief that resilience stems from optimism. While it is unpopular to deny that optimism is helpful, optimism *only* contributes to resilience when it does not distort reality.

In the Apollo 13 story, the speed with which the astronauts acted was not pessimistic, it was practical. The astronauts had a grasp on reality.

Truly resilient people share an ability to do the grueling work of "staring down" reality. They have a down-to-earth view of the parts of reality that matter most for survival.

Victor Frankl, a well-known survivor of a German concentration camp, wrote one of the most influential books of the 20th century. In *Man's Search for Meaning,* he describes how he confronted his reality head on, even in the most dehumanizing of circumstances. Facing that reality, and owning the things he could control, enabled him to fare better than those who relied on optimism alone. Research on other prisoners of war validates Frankl's experience.

Staring down reality allows us to sort through what we *can* and *cannot* change. It leads to accountability and ownership of results. A firm grasp on reality also helps us to understand the aspects of an issue to which we might otherwise be blind. With that perspective, we train ourselves to survive.

Frankl and the Apollo 13 astronauts were in extreme situations, but the premise is true for all of us: In extreme adversity, looking through rose-colored glasses with forced optimism can spell disaster. Optimism has its place, but alone, it is not enough.

2. A deep belief that what you're doing is **MEANINGFUL**

Coutu also says that, "Meaning can be elusive and just because you found it once doesn't necessarily mean you'll keep finding it again. This directs us to the importance of values, which are the glue that holds resilient companies together during down-turns. Values are more important for organizational resilience than having resilient people on the payroll. Strong values infuse an environment with meaning because they offer ways to *interpret and shape* events. Making meaning is how resilient people build bridges from present-day hardships to a fuller, better constructed future."

Resilient people and organizations seek meaning, even in terrible times. When the acceptance of reality is missing, this becomes extremely difficult.

Frankl came to realize the importance of finding meaning in the face of suffering because doing so transformed painful experiences into resilience to keep going long past when he wanted to give up.

He found meaning by stepping outside of the situation and looking back at it. It certainly didn't mean he suffered any less, but it did mean that he made an intentional choice to apply a different filter, thereby mining meaning from his experience. He focused on the impact of his situation on mankind and became determined to capture every thought to tell his story.

Adopting the mindset of a victim, however justified, can prevent us from accepting reality, which makes it difficult to find meaning in hurtful events. Making meaning, however, is critical to integrating the learnings from our experiences, so we can grow and emerge stronger and more effective.

When we *own* our reality, and squeeze meaning from it, we empower ourselves to improvise in the moment for best results in the future.

3. An uncanny ability to **IMPROVISE**

Resilient people improvise. They think fast and on their feet. It is one of their most powerful assets and defines their ability to succeed no matter what the situation, whether it is an ad-libbing comedian, a quarterback changing a play at the line of scrimmage, or a corporate leader redirecting the company when a market disruptor emerges. Resilient people can improvise because they have a framework or set of tools at their disposal that they practice and know how to use.

The NASA crew for Apollo 13 put together a set of common implements that enabled them to duplicate the original equipment that had been destroyed on the spacecraft. Perhaps the most resourceful of those duplications was the rebuilding of an oxygen hose using plastic bags, cardboard, and duct tape. It was all they had available to them and the team's ingenuity worked. The lessons and the breakthroughs that team created changed space travel forever—way beyond bouncing back.

The ability to improvise requires small, daily, in-the-moment decisions to solve problems without the usual or obvious tools. If you have seen the T.V. show *MacGyver* or have been on a team where you've been given more work, but no additional headcount, you know what I mean. The Hindi word "jugaad" reflects this idea well.

Improvisation requires creative, solution-focused thinking. It means making do with what you have and doing more than you thought you could with the resources available to you. It is the ability, determination and grit to solve a situation using whatever means necessary.

We tend to make light of the ability to improvise and doing so can even be humorous. But make no mistake: This skill often determines our resilience.

Technical and Adaptive Challenges

Most athletes spend about 90% of their time training to be able to perform at peak levels 10% of the time. For example, professional football players train six days a week to play one game on Sunday. Business leaders are a different story. We are expected to perform 90% of the time with much less than 10% of our time spent training or recovering. It rings true that the most overworked athlete in the world is the corporate executive. As a result, leaders become burned out, making them less able to withstand disruption when it strikes.

Resilience is demonstrated by the pro quarterback who keeps his head in the midst of a two-minute drill, driving his team down the field with opposing players hurling their bodies at him in the overwhelming din of a roaring crowd, with maybe the entire season on the line.

Resilience is required of the corporate executive who must enter a conference room in a moment of company crisis, address his or her team after a major financial jolt that is threatening the very core of the company, and provide inspirational support and a plan to save the day. All of this, while wondering, "How do I tell my family I'll be late for dinner again?"

Corporate "athletes" can build resilience muscles to enable us to withstand more and come back stronger, particularly in today's business landscape of constant, chaotic change. According to Coutu, highly resilient executives develop stress-resistant behaviors. They deal well with adversity while synthesizing valuable lessons from their experience that allow them (and their organizations) to recreate themselves to be stronger, better-equipped and more effective.

More importantly, they sustain better health and energy reserves under the constant pressure of intensely stressful environments.

> *"If you want something you've never had,*
> *you have to do something you've never done."*
>
> – Thomas Jefferson

The types of challenges people face in today's world, both personally and professionally, are increasingly more complex. Many require solutions that involve thinking differently–*radically* differently–than we ever have before. Often, they require understanding and reliance on an increasing array of stakeholders in ways in which we have never experienced. These are called *adaptive* challenges and they require more than the usual solutions.

The catch is that it's hard to be adaptive when we are exhausted. Anyone who works full-time and/or has children, knows that patience can wear thin by the end of the day–or even at the beginning of it.

Everyone we know deals with challenges every day.

Ron Heifetz, author and Professor at Harvard's Kennedy School of Government and founder of both the Adaptive Leadership Network and the Center for Public Leadership, defines two types of challenges:

Technical challenges – those *resolved by applying expertise*

Adaptive challenges – those *resolved by thinking differently*

An adaptive challenge represents a situation for which the solution lies outside the current way of doing things, where doing what you've always done with what you've always known won't solve the problem. According to Heifetz, "these challenges require developing new capacity –a new adaptation–that either narrows the gap between aspirations (values) and reality, or first rectifies (prioritizes) contradictory values and then narrows the gap. It may result from either an internal contradiction between the shared values people hold and the reality of their lives, or from a conflict among people over values, beliefs, or strategy."

Companies who grow by acquisition deal with these kinds of contradictions every day. When different corporate cultures come together, at some point, a new one will emerge, and some people will lose what they held dear.

Adaptive challenges are the kinds of situations that require people to make tradeoffs between values and beliefs and to mobilize people to innovate and implement solutions that can change the "game" forever.

Generally, technical challenges can be solved either by finding appropriate expertise or writing a check for it. Some examples include creating an assembly line, reengineering a process, and implementing a computer system. Many challenges have both adaptive and technical components.

For our purposes, we will focus more on the adaptive, as those are increasingly more prevalent and driving an increased need for resilient people and organizations. They tend to require more intentional and complex thought, as well as an understanding of stakeholders and ability to mobilize people.

Adaptive challenges require (paraphrased from Heifetz):

- **Learning and openness** to new ideas. This may include diagnosing or clarifying the problem in the first place because often in an adaptive challenge, the problem, work to be done, or real issue is ambiguous.

- **Tradeoffs** in loyalties, values, and behaviors, evaluating what has become expendable, giving something up, and distinguishing what must be carried forward.

- **Embracing losses** as an impetus to do things radically differently or learn new competencies.

- **Progress** outside of operational norms.

- **Shifting** problem solving from experts to a wider variety of stakeholders doing the work.

A great example of an adaptive challenge was when Steve Jobs began marketing digital music before people knew what an iPod was. Apple demonstrated extreme innovation in rolling out a product that the market had never seen or needed, yet suddenly couldn't live without.

Apply it right now

Think of some of the challenges you have faced in the past year. What are some things you have had to overcome in your personal and professional life? These can be things that happened to you or that you were a part of.

List three (3) personal and professional challenges you have faced. Examples can include things like life events (changing jobs, getting married, or moving) or they may be smaller things like starting a new project, selecting a new lawn service, or dealing with an issue with your child's teacher. It doesn't matter what kind of challenge it was.

The goal is to start thinking about which ones are adaptive and which are technical because each can benefit from different types of thinking. Some challenges may even have components of both. For example, in a household move, packing and unloading are technical, but helping your family assimilate to a new culture is quite adaptive.

See if you can identify which of the challenges you listed were **adaptive** and which were **technical** challenges and circle A or T, respectively.

Personal Challenges		Professional Challenges	
1.	A T	1.	A T
2.	A T	2.	A T
3.	A T	3.	A T

Resilience Enables Adaptive Leadership

Adaptive Leadership is the practice of mobilizing people to tackle these kinds of tough challenges and thrive in volatile, uncertain, complex and ambiguous (VUCA) environments. It describes the more difficult work needed, often to work through tradeoffs in values and acknowledge losses, particularly in times of rapid, disruptive change.

During the civil rights movement Dr. Martin Luther King Jr. demonstrated Adaptive Leadership when he mobilized a group of young people and asked the country to examine its stated values. Freedom was a core value on which the United States of America was founded, and one the country prided itself on, yet, as Dr. King pointed out, it was a value that was not afforded to every citizen. It was this disorienting dilemma that drove the civil rights movement. Dr. King's ability to mobilize people – calling attention to the real issue, causing people to question things they held dear, and driving progress that changed a nation–is a resounding example of Adaptive Leadership.

"The single most common source of leadership failure we've been able to identify–in politics, community life, business, or the nonprofit sector–is that people, especially in positions of authority, treat adaptive challenges like technical problems."

– Heifetz & Linsky

Here's the challenge: Adaptive challenges require *radically different thinking* about how to elevate and energize people to thrive in the face of fast-paced change, more so than anything most of us have been taught. Most of these challenges will not be solved by generations of management training that taught us how to delegate, "manage up," hold people accountable, and create structures and processes into which work fits.

While older command-and-control paradigms are still useful in certain contexts, a different approach, Adaptive Leadership, is a more effective response to the speed and necessity with which adaptive challenges are turning our world, and our businesses, upside down.

Vulnerability Does Not Mean Weak

Vulnerability plays a huge role here.

Vulnerability is, essentially, the willingness to appear less than adequate. It is critical for authenticity and is a requirement for both resilience and adaptive leadership. And shame blocks vulnerability. Brene Brown, best-selling author and Research Professor at the University of Houston describes shame as toxic. "Shame causes us to think and rethink until we don't know what's true and who we are anymore." When it is not safe to be vulnerable, shame wins.

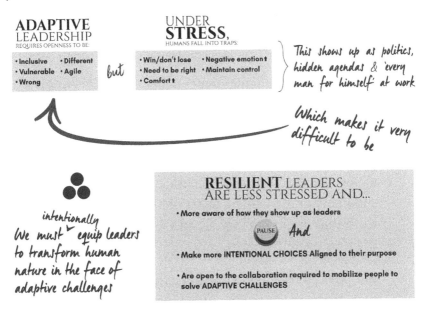

The Case for Resilience in Organizations
Presented to the Adaptive Leadership Network
at Harvard's Kennedy School of Government October 2017

No one leads well like that.

The graphic above, presented at Harvard's Kennedy School's Adaptive Leadership Network Conference in 2017 by Jennifer Eggers, links the research of several leading researchers (Ron Heifetz, Marty Linsky, Bob Kegan and Chris Agyris) and illustrates the link between resilience and adaptive leadership. This gets to the heart of who we are both as individuals and organizations.

When we cannot –or are not willing to– be vulnerable we cannot lead effectively. Adaptive leadership requires a willingness to be wrong coupled with an openness to revolutionary innovation.

Transformative ideas may come from anywhere. If we are reluctant to be wrong, those ideas may never see the light of day.

The catch (and a good reason for the LeaderShift® Resilience Framework) is that when under stress, Harvard professor Chris Argyris' research tells us that all human beings, even leaders, fall into the same traps that derail our performance.

- Highly stressed people don't collaborate well; they focus on being right. We fight to be right and avoid being wrong, to a point that we close off an open exchange of ideas.

- When faced with difficult conversations, we strive to maximize comfort and minimize negative emotions. We sugarcoat or ask leading questions so we can avoid telling the truth that might hurt someone's feelings, or that might raise the tension in the room.

- We fight to maintain control to the point that it diminishes our ability to hear the other person or understand their perspective.

In corporations, these traps show up as politics, hidden agendas, and "every man/woman for themselves." They make it extremely difficult for leaders to mobilize people effectively enough to advance solutions to adaptive challenges.

Adaptive Leadership requires not only inclusivity and vulnerability, it also demands that we invite other points of view to diagnose and solve complex and ambiguous problems with solutions that we may not have tried before. It requires openness to the possibility that we might be wrong or uninformed, and it requires pivoting when a solution comes from a place we might least expect. When stress causes us to cling to control or being right, it is very difficult to be inclusive. It's not our fault. It's human nature. We succumb to it no matter what race, color, religion, country or socioeconomic background we were raised in. But it is our problem.

Here's an example of Adaptive Leadership and resilience in action:

* * * * *

Large retail companies rely on new store openings to lift sales. Several years ago, a major auto parts retail store had an impressive goal to open over 300 new stores. Its commitments to Wall Street were aggressive and relied on that lift.

But by July of that that year, it was apparent that with only 250 stores planned, the New Stores Team was not going to meet the goal. They hadn't found enough locations that met their criteria. In an increasingly competitive market combined with the rapid growth of a major competitor, this could have created a deadly blow. You can imagine the conversation between the head of New Stores and the leadership team.

In reality, that conversation sounded very different from what you probably imagined. There was no debate, no arguing and no visible scramble. With minimal drama, and with astounding speed, the entire company pulled itself together.

A well-aligned bonus structure was responsible for this degree of collaboration. Not meeting the sales goal as a company not only threatened the company's stock price; it stood to impact every single employee's income. Instead of pointing fingers, placing blame and giving up, every employee at every level jumped in to find a way to meet the sales goal without the new stores. Brainstorming sessions were held in every department. Sales ran incentives, Marketing ran promotions, and Supply Chain stepped it up. Even HR found creative ways to bring on better talent and accelerate training that drove sales.

The company met its goals that year because its leaders quickly mobilized people across the entire organization to think creatively and pick up the slack. Many areas traded the plans they had made and made sacrifices for the broader goal. Heroes emerged where they were least expected.

Because of significant planning and an effort to get everyone on the same page, there was crystal-clear alignment to delivering the goal, so that when things got tough there was no question as to how to proceed. Everyone pulled together.

Bonus paid out at 100% that year to almost every employee. That's an adaptive and resilient organization.

When we are asked to help organizations increase their resilience, there are two factors on which we focus: a **clear Resilience Framework** for every employee and the company; **and laser-like alignment** to a clearly articulated strategy.

Every person, every priority and every investment must all be aligned to the goal. There can be no question about what is most critical. By the time you need that kind of alignment in a crisis, building it is too late.

This book provides a framework that can be applied to building both personal resilience and individual resilience. The framework will guide the preparation required to build resilience before we need it, either for ourselves or for our teams.

There are a few foundational items we want to think about before we dive into the detail, but in the following pages, we will meet with each component of resilience, and in some cases, in an up-close and personal experience. If we follow this framework, by the end of this book, a clear plan will emerge for how to build the resilience required to both lead and participate in adaptive challenges and to be energized and elevated instead of knocked down and fatigued when life and work get tough.

Resilience IS A RESULT OF:

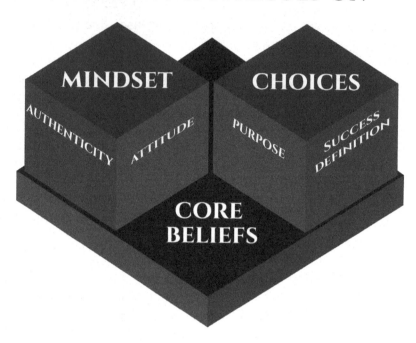

LeaderShift® Resilience Framework

The Leader*Shift®* Resilience Framework can be leveraged to build both individual AND organizational resilience. It does, however, require some learning and discipline. We have found that this learning works most effectively when the concepts and framework are applied individually first. For this reason, the remainder of this book is divided into two parts. The first is focused on applying the framework personally, and the second, to your team or organization.

Resilience is where true grit meets finesse as you jump back in the game after getting knocked to the sidelines. It's where you might eat some crow and swallow your pride because deep inside you know that moving forward fast is more important than being heard choking and you'd rather get to next than spend one more minute stuck.

Wrapping it Up

To build adaptive leaders, we must *intentionally* equip people and our organizations to evolve and intervene with more effective decisions and behaviors in the face of adaptive challenges.

Resilient people, by definition, are less stressed and:

- More aware of how they show up as leaders

- Better able to press the "pause button" in the heat of the moment

- Make more intentional choices aligned to their purpose

- Are open to the collaboration required to mobilize people to solve adaptive challenges

This enables us to build resilience in ourselves and our organizations. The point lies in building it in **both** before we need it.

Leaders who have taken the time to build resilience personally are better equipped to drive the preparation required by their teams or organizations to build resilience before they need to rely on it. Intentional preparation is required. The same preparation builds the same type of framework and it must be applied to both individuals and organizations to maximize its effectiveness.

Making It Stick

For each of the personal and professional challenges you listed in the exercise earlier, ask yourself:

- From which did you emerge stronger?

- Which of the challenges made it difficult to be as effective as you wanted to be for a while, even after the challenge was over?

- With the benefit of hindsight, how could you have been more resilient, more effective and responded faster?

Taking it With You

- Resilience can be learned.

- The characteristics of resilient people are the same as the characteristics of resilient organizations:

  ○ A firm grasp on reality in order to actively change it

  ○ A deep belief that our life and work is meaningful and necessary

  ○ The ability to improvise in the heat of the moment, on our feet

- Developing a framework for resilience, to prepare for disruptions before they happen, equips leaders at all levels to be more agile AND to mobilize people to solve adaptive challenges.

- Adaptive challenges, as opposed to technical ones, are those that require different ways of thinking, different types of behaviors, clearly embraced values, and the ability to mobilize people to solve those challenges.

PART ONE

Building Individual Resilience

LeaderShift® Resilience Framework

Resilience IS A RESULT OF:

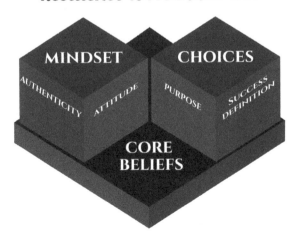

"A good half of the art of living is resilience."

– Alain de Botton

CHAPTER 2:

The First Step: Understand The Filters You Use

Resilience IS A RESULT OF:

MINDSET
CHOICES
AUTHENTICITY ATTITUDE
PURPOSE SUCCESS DEFINITION
CORE BELIEFS

"You see things, and you say "Why?"
But I dream things that never were, and I say, "Why not?"

– George Bernard Shaw

B efore we introduce the Leader*Shift*® Resilience Framework, there is a critical concept that will shape our ability to apply it.

Throughout history, visionary men and women have gone beyond the limits of what everyone else saw and forged their own success because they viewed their lives through different filters.

A lot of people saw foggy beaches in northern France. General Dwight D. Eisenhower saw a D-Day invasion. People marveled at the beauty of the moon at night. John F. Kennedy said, "Let's go there!" The world was content with living without personal technology until Bill Gates and Paul Allen ignited Microsoft and now millions of people are computer-literate.

It's not about what most people see, it's what *you* see.

When we polish the filters that we use to view our lives (or our organizations) by choosing the ones that best serve us, we take visionary steps towards change. This chapter provides the foundation for us not only to understand the importance of our choice of filters, but also to empower us to choose them effectively.

Because, "why not?"

The journey to becoming resilient begins with our window to the world, the way we see, sift through, and interpret events, and our ability to extract meaning from it.

Our Window on the World

New ways of viewing lead to new ways of doing.

Let's walk through the model you see here.

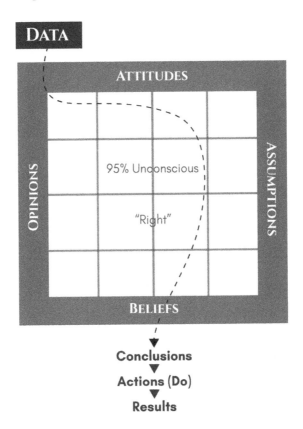

Filters: Our window on the world

We are born into this world as clean slates; absorbent sponges soaking up overwhelming amounts of information coming at us at the speed of light. Those with children know what I mean; they are learning machines. When we pride ourselves on something for which our family is known, we understand one of the earliest influences on the creation of the way we view the world and filter incoming data.

As we grow up, billions of bits of information bombard us daily, through which we sift and sort and keep that which serves us in the moment, primarily for the purpose of our immediate survival.

These lenses on life, our "ways of viewing," are formed over time, shaped by our attitudes, assumptions, opinions and beliefs. These lenses filter incoming information; they become our default settings. They cement into place neural pathways and produce automatic responses. Our ability to reframe a situation proactively, rather than resenting it, is primarily what equips us to build resilience. Our ability to do so is driven by our filters. A few examples include:

- Our gender or birth order

- Whether we went to co-ed school or same-sex school

- The number of siblings we have

- Whether our parents were divorced or stayed together

- Whether (or not) we went to university

- Whether (or not) we attended a summer camp or a church

- Whether we were bullied, neglected or abused

- Whether we were/are considered too tall/short, too fat/thin, not smart enough, or too smart, etc...

The list is endless, as are the variations on the combinations of these ways of seeing. The sum of our filters impacts the way we interact with the world around us. Well-meaning family members, friends, or teachers handed many of these filters to us. For some of us, our ancestors play a role in shaping our filters. Others we choose on our own.

Like a hard drive on our computer, our filters serve as the *operating system* on which all the apps run. If the operating system is not effective, the apps will never run as well as they could. Ever had someone send a new tricked-out PowerPoint deck on a laptop with an old version of the software? Things just don't look right. Our filters are our personal operating systems on which every decision or interpretation we make, conscious or unconscious, relies.

We become accustomed to seeing things a certain way, and because of that, we block out pertinent information and skew the incoming data to fit what we already believe and want to be right about. We do it naturally. We *all* do it. It's human nature, but it inhibits a solution focus because we are operating on the data we accept to be "real" while discarding other "facts." And most of the time (experts estimate up to 95% of the time), we're doing this unconsciously.

Our filters can also be responsible for arguments. We've all felt strongly about something ourselves and not quite known why. And we dig in our heels and try to back up our perspective. No one wants to live or work with someone who's *always* right, about everything, all the time.

Think of an infant who gets positive reinforcement from his parents when he says "please" or "thank you." He learns over time that saying please and thank you buys him approval from people in positions of perceived authority. As the years pass, this opinion that saying please and thank you is a good thing now becomes an attitude, finally hardening into an assumption that everyone *should* say please and thank you. Finally, it becomes a belief that doing so is not only a good thing to do, a helpful thing to do, it is also the *right* thing to do. In this innocuous case, the person would reflexively – unconsciously – judge others negatively should they not say please or thank you.

This type of reflexive thinking can cause problems when people try to enforce their particular filters on others with whom they live or work. "This is my belief, and therefore it's the right way to feel/think/behave, and you are wrong for not doing/thinking feeling the way I do." Thinking that way and imposing it on others does not build high-performing teams.

As this book was being written, I found myself in the hot seat, debriefing a leadership failure case in front of a room with Ron Heifetz at Harvard's Kennedy School of Government as part of an Adaptive Leadership Advanced Practitioner's retreat. At the time, I was certain that I understood my filters, or at least where they came from. As we discussed a case where I had failed, Ron asked, "Jennifer, what led you to choose hope over common sense?" I gulped and choked on my pride, realizing that I had no idea why, in this case, I had seemingly gone into "autopilot" and not asked a client an incredibly obvious question.

With Ron's help, I discovered that the situation had triggered a deep-rooted set of family values that I had never articulated. I come from a family of "scrappers." My grandfather fed his family during the depression running a gang. My father made a living doing things he was told were impossible. I recognized that I, too, am triggered by a filter that tells me to jump into action and "prove them wrong" when told I cannot do something. In this case, that was not my smartest move. Had I been aware of that filter, I could have made a different choice in the moment.

Filters can impact us destructively when we least expect them.

Our filters can force us to behave in ways that prevent personal effectiveness and professional advancement. As soon as you think you've done the work to uncover them all, there will be more. Becoming self-aware is a life-long endeavor.

Over time–psychologists say by the age of 15 or so–we have formed most of the personal beliefs that either serve to move us forward or that will hold us back, unless we intentionally choose filters that will serve us in a particular situation. We can only do that if we're aware of what they are. Without an awareness of our filtration system (also known as our perspectives and biases), we will stay "stuck" in places we don't want to be.

And here's the thing: we like to be right about our filters, whether they're helping or hurting us, or others, which is a little perverse, but then, so is the human organism.

* * * * *

A young woman, newly married, was preparing a pot roast dinner for her husband. Before she put the roast in the pan, she cut off one inch of meat from both ends. Watching her, the husband asked why she did that. It seemed like a waste of some good meat.

"Because that's the way my mother cooked it," she told him. Curious, the young woman called her mother and asked her why she always cut off an inch of meat from both ends of her pot roasts. Her mother responded, "Because that's the way my mother prepared it." Both women were now curious, so the mother called her mother and asked why she cut off the ends of the roast. The grandmother replied, "Because it wouldn't fit in my pan!"

"Right ways" are often the result of out-dated needs.

* * * * *

Welcome to the evolution and creation of confirmation biases.

By the time we are adults, working in the real world, the way we filter incoming information, or the window through which we view the world, is based on our experiences. Our experiences shape our:

- Opinions–what we like or don't

- Attitudes–the positions we take (or won't)

- Assumptions–what we *think* is true or not without actual proof

- Beliefs – what we *know* (or think we know) to be true about the world and our place in it

These four sets of filters form the basis of our belief structure, and our belief structure predetermines the results we create professionally and personally, because we carry these beliefs with us and apply them *everywhere*. Unfortunately, we're unaware of most of them. These are the essential beliefs about who we are, what we can expect from the world, and how we fit into it. This applies to our jobs, our roles and our relationships.

We carry our filters with us everywhere we go.

If we're aware of these beliefs and how they color our interactive responses, we can select the filters that help us, and those around us, and learn how to reframe the ones that hold us back.

> *Your resilience is determined by your mindset*
> *and the choices you make, both of which*
> *are driven by your core beliefs.*

Our core beliefs, the sum of all our filters, are revealed in what we say and do. It is the same for our organizations. It would be helpful to figure them out since they predict the future.

Here are just a few examples of **undermining beliefs** (restrictive/destructive) versus *resilient beliefs* (constructive/creative) and examples of the indicating behaviors:

Undermining Beliefs

Behavior Demonstrated	Words Uttered	Beliefs Held
Interrupting	*Yes, but...*	I know best/I'm afraid I might not
Lack of initiative	*I can never get ahead.*	Life is out to get me/I've been cheated
Not speaking up	*Who cares? Doesn't matter, anyway.*	My voice doesn't count/I don't feel heard
Micro-managing	*You gotta' watch your back...*	People aren't to be trusted
Non-assertiveness	*I guess...would it be okay if...*	My opinion doesn't matter
Dismissiveness/lack of empathy	*The meeting starts when I arrive. Get over it!*	My time is more important

Resilient Beliefs

Behavior Demonstrated	Words Uttered	Beliefs Held
Active listening, non-defensive communication in the face of disagreement	*I'm open to it/I'm all ears– Make your case– Tell me why you think that. What do you think?*	I can disagree and still remain open to dissenting opinions
Taking on a difficult task voluntarily	*I'll give it a shot*	I am a capable person/ the resources I need will be there
Clear, confident communication	*Let me clarify what I meant; Do you have any questions?*	My opinions matter; my voice deserves to be heard
Facing team obstacles with positivity	*No worries, I/we can handle this*	I trust myself and you (team members)
Taking time out to acknowledge feelings	*Everything okay? You look a little upset/sad, etc.*	Empathy is important to exercise/practice

In addition, our bodies don't assist us in choosing helpful filters in stressful moments. When something sudden or unexpected happens, or when we experience something dangerous to our emotional or intellectual safety, like an argument, our bodies go into fight or flight mode preparing for battle at the first sign of danger (or stress). Physically, we are hard-wired to react instantly to avoid stress, based on the filters we have established.

We've all experienced this in organizations when management, collectively, resorts to "the way we've always done things" or "how we did it last time" when disruption hits the organization, but a more innovative solution is required. Human nature applies here because organizations are made of, well, humans. Inherently, people don't like to trade the known for the unknown; change can be uncomfortable– or exciting. Or both. It's a choice that our filters drive.

Your Best Friend and Worst Enemy

Let's turn our attention for a moment to a bit of history regarding the evolution of the human brain. The threats and stressors we deal with today have evolved faster than our anatomy. To build resilience, we need to understand what we are dealing with.

There are three parts of the brain and they are developed in this order:

1. The reptilian brain stem, which governs automatic operations

2. The mammalian (also called limbic brain), which governs feelings

3. The neo cortex, which governs cognitive and creative thinking

Long ago and far away, when humans wore fur skins and hunted to survive, the **mammalian part** of our modern-day brains began to form. It is called the mammalian brain because all mammals developed it. There are three essential characteristics of the mammalian brain:

- **They care for their young**

   Reptiles do not care for their young; they eat them. People who keep snakes as pets and say "oh, he loves me," do not understand the reptilian brain. It is responsible for all automatic functions (breathing, blinking, and heartbeat) but feels no emotion whatsoever. A snake is incapable of the kind of affection that dogs and cats feel.

- **They engage in play**

   Dogs, cats, horses, and all other mammals can both play and show affection. Have you ever watched a pair of river otters? Otters know how to have fun just for the sake of enjoyment.

- **They are capable of vocalizing and displaying emotion**

  When a dog greets its owner when he or she returns home, they display happiness, tail wagging uncontrollably. Conversely, when a dog gets into the trash and is confronted, they generally show shame or sadness because they are aware they did something that displeased their human. (Cats may know they did something wrong, but the shame doesn't seem to bother them one bit.)

In the center of the mammalian brain exists a tiny little almond-shaped ganglion called the **amygdala**. It is our body's "security system" that evolved to protect us from predators, and when it is activated, we feel fear. If we never felt fear, we would end up in some dangerous places and probably hurt ourselves.

In his best-selling book *The Gift of Fear,* Gavin de Becker, a leading authority on security and violence, explains how we can learn to trust the inherent "gift" of our "gut instincts" to avoid harm by recognizing warning signs and precursors to violence. Fear is a valuable instinct that protects us and helps us learn. Hence our inherent "fight, flight, or freeze" responses.

The last part of the brain to develop was the **neocortex,** or grey matter, where critical thinking, including judgment and impulse control, occurs.

Why does the evolution of the brain matter to resilience?

Because feelings flash first, before thinking kicks in. Because, in a crisis, the amygdala shuts down rational thinking. It wins, period, at least at the beginning.

When a human is chased by a bear, reason takes flight and fear takes over, propelling us to run away, or stand glued to the ground, or pick up a stick and try to fight the bear off. Blood rushes away from our brains and into our hearts and limbs to increase our ability to run. This is why we feel our hearts pound under stress.

Even though most of us are no longer hunted by predators in today's world, the amygdala still acts as a warning system, often sounding the alarm in unwanted moments.

Have you ever been cooking bacon and suddenly your smoke alarm goes off? In the moment, all you want to do is turn the darn bell off. It's not a real fire; it's a false alarm. All you were doing was cooking bacon. Your alarm doesn't know the difference. And neither does our amygdala. It starts sounding when we're in a meeting and the bully from the department we struggle with questions our judgment in front of everyone. Our amygdala doesn't discriminate when we feel threatened.

When we start a new job or enter a situation for which we're not prepared, or in which we feel inadequate, the amygdala sends us a message through our feelings: *"Be careful."* Then, our thoughts about the situation kick in and either go to bolster or placate our fear, *depending on our filters.*

Organizations don't have an amygdala, but they are run by people who do. When a company is under stress (not making the numbers, for example), what happens? Often, corporate leaders react and begin cutting costs. First on the chopping block is usually training as all resources are focused on sales. This may help achieve numbers in the short-term, but eventually, it catches up.

In an interview many years ago, Albert Einstein was asked: "What is the most important question mankind needs to address?"

Einstein's response was not about a problem mankind faced, but rather a perspective mankind might want to develop.

His reply: "The most important question for each individual–man or woman–to be able to answer for themselves is, '**Is the universe a friendly place?**'"

That's an important question. Our answer to that question is an example of a *primary filter* for the way in which we make decisions.

Many people believe the world is not a safe place, and they have the data to back it up: war, hunger, genocide, sexual abuse, and their personal experience. The list is endless. Yet, many others believe the universe is an inherently friendly place and they can find plenty of data to support their point of view: a newborn baby, strangers who help in times of crisis, volunteers who lend a hand, flowers blooming in a meadow. Their list is endless too.

We can be right about any damn thing we want to be right about.

> *"There are two ways to live your life.*
> *One is as though nothing is a miracle.*
> *The other is as though everything is a miracle."*
>
> – Albert Einstein

We can choose to reframe the world around us. Rather than holding the filter, "the universe is out to get me," we can choose an alternative belief that "the universe is here to help me." This subtle shift can have a huge impact on our lives and those around us.

The question I pose is always, "What do you want to be right about?" Is it that your boss is a *jerk?* Or is it that he's doing the best he knows how and is uninformed about this topic? Which choice of filter will elicit the healthiest response in your interactions with your boss?

Every single person we know has an amygdala. We are all, at our core, emotional beings with the same innate stress response. The degree to which we understand how to influence our feelings and responses will determine how well we leverage them in ways that serve us best, drive results and come back faster, energized and elevated by setbacks.

A Filter Worth Adopting

We have a radical suggestion to make. We suggest you adopt a filter that says, "Life is hard."

Why would we make that suggestion? Not because it's a fun thing to believe, but because it will help you and your team drive better results and more fulfillment. Period.

This has nothing to do with optimism or pessimism, or whether your glass is half empty or half full. It's about "facing down reality" – Coutu's first ingredient in the resilience recipe. Adopting the filter that "life is hard" is a very down-to-earth and proactive point of view.

We can believe life is inherently good, or not. We can believe anything we want. But if we believe life (or our company) "owes" us something, or that troubles, disruption, rapid change and loss or pain are things we shouldn't have to experience, then we are setting ourselves up for a hard fall.

"In this life you will have troubles." This sounds like a song title, but it is a Biblical quote from Jesus of Nazareth. The scriptures do not say you *might* have troubles or that some people do. They proclaim that we *all* do. If you are not Christian, or if a mention of the Bible turns you off, pick any other faith's sacred book. Regardless of your religious perspective–whether it be Christian, Jewish, Hindi or Buddhist–this is one thing that almost every ideology agrees on: "In this life you will have troubles."

Does anyone you know *not* have troubles? Have you known anyone who worked at a company that was never challenged?

Admittedly, some people have more troubles than others, but what we go through is measured against our own experiences, so the level of the challenge or trouble is subjective. It cannot be meaningfully compared with someone else's.

M. Scott Peck states the same position in the first paragraph of his seminal book, *The Road Less Traveled*: "Life is difficult." He continues: "It is a great truth, one of the greatest truths. It is a great truth because once we truly see this truth, we transcend it.

> *"Once we truly know that life is difficult – once we truly understand and accept it – then life is no longer difficult. Because once it is accepted, the fact that life is difficult no longer matters."*
>
> – M. Scott Peck

It is the way we rise in the face of our individual troubles, or our organizational troubles, or our industry's troubles, that determines how resilient we become. Troubles or stressors can be opportunities too, depending on our filters. We recommend adopting the filter "Life is hard" because it works. It's empowering. Far from prompting a pessimistic position, it puts us in a place to find meaning in adversity immediately because we expect it and are ready for it, everywhere we go.

We chose the job we're in as well as our relationships. Meaning is there for the making. It's there for the finding. But it requires a choice to look. It requires effort.

"Life is hard" is a down-to-earth point of view. It is a lot like saying there are eight ounces of water in a sixteen-ounce glass, instead of, "it's half full," or "it's half empty." This is neither optimistic or pessimistic and it has nothing to do with being a victim.

Instead of asking "Why me?" the filter, "life is hard" is about asking *"Why NOT me?"* It calls us to ask, "If me, then how can I stare it down, diagnose it, and hold space for it to get better while I figure out how to squeeze some meaning from it?"

Life may be hard. It can also be good. The two beliefs are not mutually exclusive.

Why is Life Hard?

We have all kinds of technical gadgets that make our lives easier. Humans no longer plow the fields and harvest the grain. We have machines that do it for us. We no longer ride our horse to town; we get into our cars or jump aboard public transportation. We no longer work a water pump handle or make candles for light at night. But—and this is a *big* but—life is harder on an *emotional* level because it's moving faster. We are bombarded with information in a myriad of media and the evolution of the human brain has not kept pace.

The kinds of challenges we deal with today are exponentially more complex than they were even two years ago. This is largely because of the increasing pace and levels of change, advancements in technology, and the degree to which people are more connected and have access to information. When more people have a voice, they expect to be heard and have a say. More voices are useful when solving complex challenges, but they can also make solving issues more complicated.

There is nothing about the future that is as certain as it once seemed to be. In some ways, it's also because we are trying to be ourselves in a world that seeks to make us someone else—someone who will "fit in" to this organization or that family or educational system.

Bottom line: Try it. Look at what happens every day through a lens of, *"Life is hard."* It may be counterintuitive, but it will make our lives easier. We might even find ourselves feeling grateful more often that things are not half as hard as we thought they would be. The irony, described by Peck, is that as soon as we accept that life is difficult, it suddenly ceases to be so hard. Reframing the filter helps us clearly see reality so we can confront it and overcome its challenges.

Just as we have filters that shape how we view and respond to the world, *so does every other person* with whom we live and work. And as much as our filters are, of course, the *right* ones, everyone else thinks theirs are, too. When stress kicks in—and in today's world, no matter the industry, stress is rampant—it's hard to be ourselves and live up to everyone else's expectations when our amygdala is screaming, *"Danger, danger!"*

Even in the most upsetting circumstances, there is, however, one thing we can always do: Push the "pause button" long enough to choose a more effective response despite our anxiety.

Breathing Benefits

When that *"glump"* in your stomach happens, or the blood drains from your face, or you can't get started on that presentation that is due tomorrow because you can't seem to focus, here's the first and best thing to do: BREATHE.

Consider the "rule of threes" of human survival: we can, on average, survive three weeks without food, three days without water, and only three minutes without oxygen.

So, when we talk about our need to breathe, we're talking about our most immediate survival mechanism. And what's the first thing to be affected in the face of stress? Our breathing.

When we sense an incoming threat, whether that threat is physical, emotional, or intellectual – and whether it is real or imagined–the amygdala is activated, and your body responds exactly the same way as everyone else's, every single time. When that automatic fight-flight-freeze self-preservation mechanism begins, here's what happens inside your body in order:

1. The focus narrows to include data coming only from the perceived threat. All non-pertinent information is pushed outside.

2. Capillaries tighten, causing hands and feet, ears and nose, to grow cold in the face of reduced oxygen as the blood flow in our bodies gets redirected to our major muscle groups in preparation for fight-flight. We don't need a warm nose when running from a bear (or the boss); we need more blood, and the oxygen it carries, in the quads and butt.

3. Our hearts start beating faster, sending more blood more quickly. We have all experienced feeling as if our hearts were going to burst out of our chests when we first stood in front of a large audience, or went on our first interview, or said "I love you" for the first time. And, it happens in an instant! *Boom-boom-boom.*

We might label it as being nervous or anxious or upset, but let's call it what it is: Fear. In that moment, some aspect of our survival is being threatened. And it seems to happen through no choice of our own; the 95% unconscious operating system takes over.

The key to clearer thinking becomes recognizing the signs indicating that our amygdala has been activated. In the recognition that the alarm has sounded, we have an opportunity to *breathe*. One long deep breath can provide immediate relief in stressful moments. We can't *talk* fear down from the ledge. It's impossible. We breathe it down from the ledge. Talking comes *after* breathing.

Once we've taken one deep breath, we are better able to assess the situation. We have neutralized the threat whether it is a bear or Fred from Finance who frowned when you answered his question. *Boom-boom-boom.*

BREATHE.

Take one deep breath.

It's like pushing an invisible, internal "pause" button, and it redirects blood flow from our legs to our brain. In that moment, we need oxygen in our brain, and we need it fast. Only deep breathing will get it there in time to collect our thoughts.

And, *then* talk. We will make more sense to ourselves and to everyone around us.

First, ask yourself: What did you just see or hear, and then, what caused you to feel alarmed or nervous?

Fred from Finance frowned.

What does a frown mean? *Confusion, disapproval?*

Do you know what *his* frown is all about?

No.

So, after a deep breath, and with a clearer head, you speak to Fred,

"You're frowning."

You have stated a fact, only. What you observed. Then you ask him, "Do you have a question? Is something I said unclear? Or do you disagree?"

You don't panic, get intimidated or back down. You simply request clarification. And, the beauty of all this? It only took ten seconds.

And your heart is beating normally again.

A Side Note on Feelings

Our feelings are simply messengers. They are porters of information that should not be ignored, even in the workplace. Displays or acknowledgment of negative emotions are often culturally taboo or frowned upon. However, they are ever-present and guide most of our choices, whether we admit it or not. They are like electric cords running under the carpet, potentially unseen, but there, nonetheless.

Whether we are aware of them consciously or not, emotions play a powerful and fundamental role. Feelings are neither good nor bad. They are just involuntary, socialized responses to a situation. Learning what they are, and why they occur, and when they occur for us, becomes critical to effective self-control.

Without self-awareness, there is no self-control. Without self-control, there can be no advancement.

Wrapping it Up

Filters matter.

What we see and hear is filtered such that we inevitably confirm our current beliefs. Noticing the effects of the filters we have chosen in our lives and our organizations is the first step to developing our ability to bounce back better after a setback.

Resilience is not about putting things back the way they were. It is about finding a *new normal* –moving forward, getting comfortable and collaborating with other people again. It's about being able to be energized and elevated by disruption, instead of being crushed by it.

Remember: Leadership requires extreme self-knowledge. We had better be able to figure out what we believe, and why, before we ask any member of a team to follow us into a turbulent sea of uncertainty.

Making it Stick

Make a list of some of the behaviors or ways of thinking you know you do, that get in the way of you producing your best effort. Use the examples below to get you started. Then see if you can uncover the supporting belief.

You might find that the belief is built on an unrealistic expectation of yourself or others. Unfortunately, we have all been steeped in a culture of expected perfection.

Know this: Perfection doesn't exist.

But your resilient self, your best self, does. And the only way to uncover it is to do a little digging.

What I do (that is ineffective):	Why I do it (Identify underlying rationale, beliefs):
Examples:	*Examples:*
• *I refrain from voicing an opinion*	*…Because I believe things should have a logical flow*
• *I get frustrated and start to shut down when someone speaks in an unstructured manner*	*…Because I don't have the time nor the patience to listen*
• *I get irritated and brusque in my communication and sometimes I check my phone too often*	*…Because I have to be in the loop, and a good boss is supposed to know everything*
• *I stop for a drink on the way home*	*…Because I need help taking the edge off*

Ask Yourself:

1. What are some of the filters you know you have that shape how you take in and interpret information?

For example, a woman with a domineering father may believe she should defer to older men, a youngest child may believe others will step in to fix problems first, or a person who has not been exposed to another ethnicity or faith may believe things they were told about "those people," whether good or bad.

2. What are some of the filters you see in your organization whether they are articulated and discussed or not?

    For example, "don't disagree with the boss," "penny-wise or pound foolish" or "we will be the first to market even if what we have is not perfect."

3. What are some filters you could select to help you achieve a more effective outcome?

    For example, "I am welcome here," "I have earned the right to speak on this topic" or "I choose to trust until others prove me wrong"

Taking it With You

-   Our filters and our beliefs construct our window on the world. The way we interpret things reflects what we believe.

-   What do you want to be right about? Choose your answer carefully.

-   Choose the filter that "Life is Hard." Along with, "Life is Good." These filters don't need to compete, in fact, they can complement each other.

-   The way we perceive what happens around us predetermines our response to it. If we view it as threatening, we will go into defense/attack mode, but if viewed as an opportunity/ challenge, we can shift into learning mode.

-   When our amygdala is activated and our internal smoke alarm sounds: BREATHE.

-   This immediate response to the danger signal redirects oxygen from our large muscle groups back to our brains where we need it most in times of stress.

CHAPTER 3:

Create A Mindset To Minimize Stress: Authenticity And Attitude

*"Authenticity is the alignment of head, mouth, heart, and feet:
thinking, saying, feeling, and doing
the same thing – consistently.*

– Lance Secretan

The Resilience Framework was born on a beach. By then, my team and I had built RapidOD, one of the fastest and most effective ways to create alignment around a business model and restructure an organization. The approach was selling itself, helping leaders and teams get aligned and greatly minimizing the pain and disruption of corporate restructuring. The Influence Workshop (an introduction to adaptive leadership and the conversations it requires) had taken off and between consulting projects and workshops, we were slowly changing how leaders think about leadership. But I was exhausted.

I needed a break, hence, the beach. But I couldn't ignore a nagging voice that kept whispering, "You missed your story."

I had been knocked down enough that people frequently asked me how I kept coming back from setbacks. By then I had rebounded from a car accident that had taken me out of competition as a nationally ranked competitive waterskier and another that took me out of training, only to be diagnosed with a condition precluding me from ever again doing cardio exercise.

That diagnosis almost broke me.

Then, after building a company and losing it (and nearly everything else) in 2009, making an empowering decision to escape an abusive relationship, being downsized from a corporate job, and diving head first out of a flaming vehicle, and five or six other major health incidents, I kept coming back, albeit with a few scars, but stronger than ever before.

How was I able to regroup and keep going again and again without becoming a victim of defeat?

That was the story the little voice was telling me I had missed. Somewhere in my personal story was something that would help others even more than RapidOD. And so I looked up and asked for some inspiration.

I had limped to the beach with my foot in a cast. Without a notebook, I grabbed a stick and began to write in the sand as it began to make sense.

Thriving when life is hard is the result of our mindset and the choices we make. Mindset is a function of our authenticity and attitude. The choices we make are a function of how we define success and purpose. The foundation of that is our core beliefs.

I wrote frantically as the tide came in, knowing there wasn't time to run and get a pen and paper. I had intentionally thought through all the things I jotted down many years prior. I did not become resilient by going through difficult experiences. Instead, I came out of my difficult experiences stronger and readier for the next one because I was resilient.

And that's just part of Jennifer's resilience story. Cynthia has her own. If the authors of one book can rise after life-threatening challenges, we all can.

And, so can your organization. The thing about resilience is that once we learn to build it individually, the same skills (and it IS a set of skills) can be applied to the organization or team that we lead.

The authors' experience of coming back from personal setbacks, coupled with decades of coaching, speaking, research and consulting with leaders and organizations at all levels, has created a pretty informed point of view on resilience.

This is not about how difficult anyone else had it because pain cannot be compared. The funny thing about life, though, is that as soon as we take a stand, the first thing that hits us is everything that goes against our stand.

Resilience is no different.

There Are Two Ways to Build Resilience

The first, and certainly the most difficult, is to go through a lot of trying situations. Many people became resilient because they went through some tough challenges and learned how to survive. They came out stronger because they "had to" to come out on the other side. The problem with that is that there are other people who would be defeated or even killed by those same situations. It's risky to assume that any of us will be able to build resilience when we need it.

The second, more reliable, and less painful way to build resilience is to do the work ahead of time to prepare, so that in the moment when you need it, a resilient choice is clear and available to you.

The Leader*Shift*® Resilience Framework was designed to serve as a guide to help both individuals and organizations think *intentionally* about resilience and do the work required to build it **before we need it**. It was designed to help accelerate our ability to develop resilience so that going through tough challenges is not *how* we build it, but *why*. As we begin to build these frameworks, the "life is hard" filter acknowledges the very reason why resilience is critical.

The main premise of the Resilience Framework is:

- Resilience is a direct result of our **mindset** and the **choices** we make.

- Our **mindset** is a function of our **authenticity** and **attitude**.

- Our **choices** are a function of our **purpose** and how we **define success**, either in life or a situation.

Resilience IS A RESULT OF:

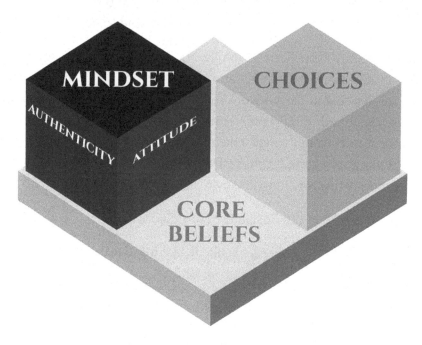

You are here: Authenticity & Attitude determine your mindset

Underlying our Mindset and Choices are a set of core beliefs. We may not know what those are right now, but to be truly resilient, we need to be able to access them. There's a good chance that even if you don't know them, they are already there, hidden in your subconscious.

Our ability to build resilience as either individuals or as organizations depends on our commitment to be intentional and aware about building the elements of this framework.

Just as the Navy SEALS prepare by carefully practicing all the necessary details of their operation to be successful on a mission, we must prepare and intentionally plan for the times when resilience will be required. We must learn how to recognize when we are being authentic, and we can learn to be intentional about our attitude by choosing our filters.

Just as some of us train in the gym to become physically stronger, we can strengthen the emotional muscles required to pause and quickly identify our purpose before walking into a firestorm. It is imperative for us to prepare and memorize a definition of success until it is so *ingrained* in the core of our being that by default, we live it. Our every choice reflects it, even when we don't have time to think about it consciously.

We can also do the difficult work of understanding our own core beliefs so that when we need to stand up in a tough situation, there is solid ground to stand on. Only then will we know we have built resilience.

Let us begin at the beginning then, with the two aspects of Mindset in the Resiliency Model: Authenticity and Attitude.

Authenticity

> *"Your authentic self is who you are when you have no fear of judgment, before the world starts pushing you around and telling you who you're supposed to be. Your fictional self is who you are when you have a mask on to please those around you."*

> – Dr. Phil McGraw

Bill Eggers ran a large division of a well-known, global, family-run provider of tree-trimming and line construction services to utility companies.

While building an electric line, one of his crews had a fatal accident. A lineman was killed as he drove a truck into the back of a load of telephone poles extending from the truck ahead of him. The driver was distracted.

The truck in front stopped, and the result was an accident so gruesome that we can't publish Bill's description.

At the time, Bill was a new Vice President. His job was largely to balance managing a group of long-time employees doing dangerous jobs with serious cost constraints, safety numbers, and pressure to increase profitability. Bill was the kind of guy who stood up for his men when it mattered, expected the best in return, and got it.

The media swarmed immediately, trying to catch someone off guard and gin up a story about a corporate giant who cut costs at the expense of safety. His own investigation was not yet complete as the media, his men and "headquarters" all looked to Bill for answers. With difficult and unanswered questions threatening the company and his new job, Bill addressed a crowd of shaken employees. At the time, he really didn't know exactly what had happened that day.

Bill explained that many of the employees would be contacted by the media. Some would be interviewed by police, attorneys, insurance companies and safety inspectors. All would be required to talk about what happened and somehow, they would need to move forward. "I have only one request," he said.

"Tell the truth."

At the time Bill didn't know if, or how badly, the truth would hurt him or the company. But he knew that anything less than authenticity in this situation was not good enough. He told his men that he didn't care how hard it was to hear or who was at fault, he wanted the truth.

That is what corporate authenticity looks like.

Unbeknownst to him at the time, when Bill placed more importance on the truth than he did on his job, or the company and any story that might have sounded better, he sent a strong message to his men and to the media: Bill and his company could be trusted.

Bill became a legend that day and he's been my business hero and mentor ever since.

Authenticity has a lot to do with self-awareness. In fact, it depends on it. Authenticity means being intentional about our image and projecting to the world who we *really* are.

Too many people live by imitation. They read about or observe good leaders and copy the habits of people they admire. The fatal flaw is that they focus on what those people *do*, rather than on how those people *think.*

This may yield short-term results, but that approach will not be sustainable. All the copying in the world will not produce the one key ingredient critical for authenticity: Knowing who we really are and making choices aligned with that knowledge.

$$* \ * \ * \ * \ *$$

As part of a business deal, a former partner sold me a Porsche at a deep discount. It wasn't a smart financial decision, but bringing it home from the west coast meant an opportunity to drive across country with my Dad and I knew those memories would be worth any cost.

While my friends may have been right about my questionable judgment for having purchased a very expensive car in the first place, I was certainly not as rich as they had decided I was. Their unwelcome attention and assumptions made me extremely uncomfortable since the image the car projected did not in any way resemble my situation. Ironically, that image represented a lot more to others than it ever did to me.

Before I bought it, I never thought about the vehicle's image. I just wanted a safe car (given two recent bad accidents) and a trip with Dad.

To make matters worse, at the recommendation of my accountant, the Porsche became a business vehicle. Because it was a capital expense, we had taken depreciation on it. That meant that in 2009, when the business failed, I could not sell the car without paying many thousands of dollars in taxes.

So, there I sat, eating ramen noodles while struggling to afford groceries, while driving around in a Porsche. The truth was that the car was paid for. It had gone down in value and I could not afford to sell it, much less buy another car. I was projecting an image that did not accurately reflect who I was. It was a "first world problem" but the stress was real, and completely unnecessary.

Minimizing unnecessary stress is reason enough to strive for authenticity, but there is a more important point to be made here. In the moment when I needed resilience the most (at the end of my financial rope), the most effective course of action would have been to apply all my discretionary energy and focus towards getting out of the mess I was in. Instead, my focus (and any help I might have received) was distracted by the need to manage an image that did not align with reality.

Many of us are not good at asking for help. I can assure you, it becomes exponentially more difficult when the image we project conflicts with what we need. To build the kind of resilience required to come through challenges better off than we were before, we must avoid anything the distracts us from dealing with the real issue in the moment. Learning to be authentic accomplishes that in spades.

"Authenticity means erasing the gap between what you firmly believe inside and what you reveal to the outside world."

– Adam Grant

Authenticity is in the Overlap

Authenticity reflects the "real you," what we truly believe or feel. We are being authentic when the image we project to the world reflects who we really are.

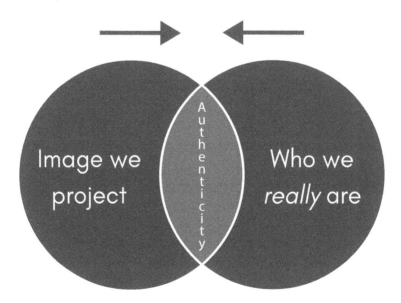

Authenticity: When the image you project reflects who you really are

In his book, *An Everyone Culture,* Bob Kegan, a professor at Harvard's School of Education, tells us that most working professionals have two full-time jobs: The first is their regular job (the one they are paid for) and the second, taking up an equal amount of time, is the additional job of managing their image and how they are perceived at work. In other words, they are trying to ensure positive impressions while avoiding negative ones.

Kegan's research suggests that efforts invested in image protection to "cover up their inadequacies, manage other people's impressions, show themselves to their best advantage, playing politics and hiding uncertainties" is the single biggest loss of resources organizations suffer every day. The total cost of this waste is staggering. Not to mention the psychological implications and the stress it causes while preventing people and organizations from reaching their full potential.

We recognize the people around us who are authentic. They have a sincerity about them that invites us to trust them. They know they are good enough without needing someone to remind them all the time. They're open to learning in just about any situation, because they're not afraid of appearing as though they don't know everything. They ask questions and show that they care about understanding the answers. They know how to manage ambiguities, and that we cannot get around life's inherent contradictions. These characteristics underscore the importance of both a willingness to be authentic – our best and highest self – and to demonstrate a healthy, proactive attitude.

Authenticity is about choosing to live without guilt and resentment. It's about treating people (including ourselves) with compassion and respect. And most of all, it's about making decisions from a place of love (in service of the highest good) rather than a place of fear (avoiding a certain fate).

Authentic people are real. Even if we don't like them, we will most likely respect them and trust their intentions, even if we don't agree with them.

Why Being Authentic Is So Critical to Resilience

When life is hard or any sort of disruption hits, we have a finite amount of energy to deal with it. Think of this as a big red tank of energy that is available for whatever is facing you. Our tanks are different sizes, based on the amount of resilience we have, but each of our tanks hold a finite amount. When the energy tank registers, "empty," it's gone. At that point, we are burned out, tired and no longer effective. We need to build resilience so there is enough extra energy in the tank when things get difficult and reserves are required.

When we are being authentic, we use a minimal level of energy. We don't have to think about how we *should* respond to things. We just respond naturally and go about our day. When the image we are projecting is not natural we expend more energy. As Kegan's research reminds us, we pause to think about our image. We adjust, measure, and gauge our reactions according to how we want to appear to others or to what is politically acceptable. All this planning and calculating, done consciously or unconsciously, drains the tank faster because it requires more energy. It also drains organizations of expendable time.

In times when we really need to be resilient, a moment of crisis, for example, we need all the reserves we can muster. There is no extra margin. With the pace of change and the complex nature of adaptive challenges, we simply cannot afford to allow managing our images to drain the tank sooner. Being aware of when we are being authentic, or not, and why, helps us find ways of being ourselves in a fashion that works for those around us. In that way we'll have the reserves left in our tanks when we need it.

Increasing our willingness to express ourselves authentically and appropriately is a critical component of building resilience.

Apply It Right Now

Jot down the first couple areas you can think of where your identity (or how others see you) does not match who you really are inside.

What I Do	Why?
Eg. I refrain from saying what I think Eg. I make up answers when I don't really know Eg. I refuse to stay home when I'm sick Eg. I shut down when the tension gets high	... because I think people will think I'm stupid ...because a good leader would have all the answers ...because half of leadership is showing up ...because it's easier than confrontation
1.	
2.	
3.	

Attitude

"For success, attitude is equally as important as ability."

– Walter Scott

When I lived in Memphis, I decided I wanted to learn how to play bluegrass music. Most of the people I played music with said that it was good for stress relief. They played to relax. I didn't. I played when I was relaxed. It turned out that the pursuit with which I had fallen in love was one of the hardest things I've ever done. And everyone else made it look effortless.

The first time I picked up the guitar, it felt flat out impossible. It was only because I had made up my mind to prove to a friend that I could learn a particularly difficult song that I kept at it.

And at it, and at it.

Then one day, I muddled through that song. And, the next day it got easier. Finally, after what had seemed like forever, I could play it all the way through correctly, slowly at first and then faster. There were times that I never believed it would be possible.

It never got easier to learn a new song. It was merely a choice I made to learn to play.

Having a good attitude doesn't always mean the glass is half full and it certainly doesn't mean we're always happy about it. Having a good attitude is about staring down reality—again, one of Coutu's characteristics of resilient people and organizations. I didn't learn the tune "Red Haired Boy" because I was cheerful. There were days I pulled my hair out. On the days I played until my fingers bled, the attitude I chose had nothing to do with being positive. It had everything to do with facing the reality that what I had chosen to learn and to invest time and energy in, was not an easy or quick endeavor. My *attitude* of determination had everything to do with the choice I made to continue.

Attitudes, though part of our filtering system, can be consciously chosen, molded, and perpetuated. But it takes effort.

Trying to explain the filter, *"Life is hard,"* is always fun when the *"rah, rah"* people (you know, the cheerleader types that are usually found in training organizations) are sitting in the front row. They tend to shake their heads and get annoyed until finally one of them will raise a hand and say that this filter is pessimistic and counter-productive. I can sense their disappointment; they cannot imagine how an adult learning expert could possibly *not* present everything in a positive light. Well, everything is not positive. And the sooner we face reality and get ahead of it, the better.

Usually shortly after that, someone tells me that my glass is half empty. It is not. There are four ounces in my glass. It is neither half full nor half empty – except by virtue of my choice.

Resilience: It's Not About Bouncing Back is not negative either. It is reality.

Elaine was an employee deep in my organization when I worked for Bank of America. I did not know her, other than by name, when I received a call from the head of our ethics and compliance department.

He gave me strict orders to fire her. Financial troubles involving employees' bank accounts were simply not tolerated. It seemed Elaine had gone over the limit on a line of credit she had with the bank.

I had no other evidence that Elaine had done anything wrong and frankly, while she didn't work directly for me, she had a fine reputation and was good at her job. Much to the chagrin of the ethics investigator, who clearly had never been challenged, I made the choice to do some investigating myself.

I learned that Elaine had taken out a small line of credit to replace some kitchen appliances years before. She had been paying on it for a long time but was surprised when she received a letter from the Bank declaring it, "Paid in Full."

Since she was surprised, and she knew a bit about how the bank worked, she asked for a full audit of her account to be certain it was, indeed, paid off. By the time she had finished telling me her story, Elaine had requested three separate audits of her account and had received four letters from the Bank stating that her line of credit had been paid off, all of which she showed me.

She and her husband were a bit confused, and each decided that the other had something to do with paying off the remainder of the loan. With all this documentation verifying that her account was in good standing, she then charged a small appliance to the same line of credit.

Three years later, the bank decided that Elaine had exceeded her line of credit, despite its approval, and that she should be fired.

"Not so fast," I told them.

My attitude has been and always will be to look after my people, even as I hold them to a high standard. Fortunately, I had a supportive boss when I refused to fire her – which could have cost me my own job - and Elaine became one of the most loyal team members I have ever had.

What I had not anticipated was the word getting out across the bank about my going to bat for Elaine. Within a few weeks, internal applications poured in and there was a fight for the open spots on my team. A few years later, when I was unjustly accused of harassment, twenty-five very diverse current and former team members stood by me.

It would have been easier and less risky for my career to do what I was told by the compliance officer, but if we don't stand by our principles when they are tested, what good are they?

If you aren't choosing your attitude. It's choosing you.

Pushing the pause button long enough to choose the most appropriate and helpful attitude in a given situation has long-term pay-offs. When we choose our attitude intentionally, it provides us an opportunity to demonstrate the best version of ourselves and propels us to become more effective authentic leaders.

Apply It Right Now

Consider the following questions:

- Can you think of a time when your attitude contributed to your ability to "face down reality?"

- How about a time when it detracted from it? Be honest and think about some of the difficult situations you have been in.

- In what situations do you tend to be overly optimistic or pessimistic?

- Do you have a "default" attitude that you seem to choose without even thinking?

Wrapping it Up

In the Leader*Shift*® Resilience Framework, we learn that resilience is a function of our mindset: our authenticity and our attitude. Our ability not only to be authentic, but also to know when we are or are not being authentic, and to own the results of both, is a skill we can practice and master over time.

Choosing our attitude (while overcoming emotions and subconscious sabotage) is also about understanding where we tend to get trapped inside our comfort zone and when and how we play it safe. We examine this more closely in the next chapter.

The speed with which we can effectively shift from the perspective that things are happening *to* us, to making choices about how we are "being" based on what is really going on, will ultimately determine our ability to build a resilient mindset.

Taking It with You

- Authenticity means being intentional about your image and projecting to the world **who you really are**.

- You know you are being authentic when the way you are perceived by others accurately reflects who you perceive yourself to be based on your values, purpose, etc.).

- Adopt the filter, "Life is hard." Not because it is true, but because it is smart.

- You either choose your attitude, or it chooses you.

CHAPTER 4

Derailers Of
A Resilient Mindset:
How Your Comfort Zone
Holds You Hostage
(And How To Break Free)

"A ship in the harbor is safe,
but that is not what ships are built for."

– William Shedd

As we look at intentionally shaping our Mindset to increase our resilience, there are a few traps to watch out for. These traps can derail our attempts to build resilience on our best day and they can sneak up on us when we least expect it. In Chapters 4 and 5, we will take an important pause to discuss them before moving on to the next component of the model (Choices).

The derailers we want to examine at this point are the constraints of our individual comfort zones and the internal emotional cancers of guilt and resentment.

Comfort Zones Can Undermine Change Efforts

"You've got to get out of your comfort zone," is a phrase we've all heard, but few know where it came from. Turns out, it's an interesting story with some less obvious lessons that rarely get talked about because of their counterintuitive nature. And the story highlights the tendency of the unconscious to exert its power in our decision making.

In the 1950's IBM commissioned a study. They wanted to find out how to best motivate their salesforce to improve sales. They hired consultants who came in and changed *everything*. They changed the color of carpets, the size of desks, the location of the walls, mixed up the departments, etc. They even shuffled the sales people to different territories and regions. They made big changes like moving high producers to low performing areas and urban sales people to rural areas.

Then, they sat back and watched to see the effects of those changes.

Here's what happened: After three months, no matter what changed, people reverted to their former patterns. A salesperson accustomed to making $50K annually suddenly found his income sliding downward and realized he would make only half of his annual income if things continued.

When this happened, the downward sliding sales people got into gear. They got motivated and brought their income back up to what they were accustomed to earning.

Why?

The guy making less money got scared. Of course, he did! We all know that feeling when money runs short. This made sense to the researchers because FEAR MOTIVATES. At least, in the short-term.

In this case, the fear at the bottom of his comfort zone represented a lower income level. He thought, "I won't be able to pay bills," "I'll have to take the kids out of private schools," "I'll have to tell my wife," or a myriad number of other concerns.

What did not make sense to the researchers was that the opposite was also true: The salesmen on track to double their salary managed to find a way (unconsciously) to sabotage their results. After three months, they were also making what they had been making prior to the changes.

Huh?

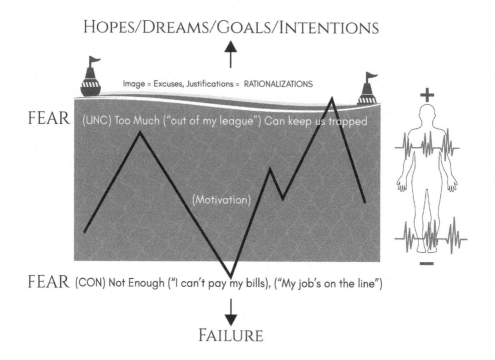

HOPES/DREAMS/GOALS/INTENTIONS

Image = Excuses, Justifications = RATIONALIZATIONS

FEAR (UNC) Too Much ("out of my league") Can keep us trapped

(Motivation)

FEAR (CON) Not Enough ("I can't pay my bills), ("My job's on the line")

FAILURE

How the Comfort Zone keeps us trapped

The researchers discovered that fear also lives at the *top* of our comfort zone, as well. In this case, for the salesmen who never seemed to make *enough* money, the fear represented him making too *much*.

Why would he be afraid of making more money?

This rationale sounded crazy to the researchers. But remember, people don't do this on purpose. They don't do it consciously. It's an *unconscious choice.*

In the first example (when the salesman wasn't making enough money), the fear was *conscious.* He saw what was happening and did whatever it took to improve his result.

But, why would someone sabotage his results, especially successful ones, even if it was done unconsciously? Some might say he felt, "out of his league" or "in over his head" or maybe he worried about living up to expectations he would not be able to maintain his increased salary. Have you ever felt like a fraud for getting a great result at something you didn't think you would be good at, or might be unable to sustain? Feeling unworthy is at the *top* of your comfort zone.

Our comfort zone is simply the space in which we feel comfortable operating, mostly because we're "used to it." That's why we say, "It's hard to teach an old dog new tricks." The IBM study showed that the top end of the comfort zone (closer to your desired outcome) kept people trapped in their particular "known zone" just as effectively as the bottom edge of their comfort zone.

We have comfort zones for every area of our life: our intimacy level in relationships, the cars we drive, the clothes we wear, the music we listen to, how much money we earn, what kinds of conversations we enjoy, how much conflict we can handle, etc. The comfort list goes on and on.

Remember that our unconscious mind:

- Has a higher processing capacity than our conscious mind

- Can performing complex tasks without conscious assistance

- Is more intuitive than the conscious mind

- Treats information as a fluid, rather than a solid - is dynamic, rather than linear

- Puts discrete pieces of information into context

- Processes subtle, unspoken messages (body language, facial expressions, communication nuances) 40,000 times faster than the conscious mind

The Comfort Zone is about our ability and willingness
to adapt to change and deal with uncertainty

We have physical, emotional, and psychological comfort zones. When we approach the top edge of one of our comfort zones and become increasingly uncomfortable (because we are about to leave our "Known Zone") we tend to offer up lots of excuses, reasons, and justifications.

We rationalize giving just a little bit less than our very best, because we're scared, so we play it safe. We get to look good to everyone else, and we get to maintain our image, the part we want others to believe of us that we don't believe of ourselves.

"Image" means making what others think of you
more important than the way you feel about yourself

Our comfort zones are constructed over time. Most of the protective boundaries we apply, like an invisible fence that shocks us when we try to cross it, are constructed or influenced by family members, teachers, and friends with the best intentions. Most of our boundaries—a result of our filters—were imposed long ago for self-protection and become coping strategies. We all use the coping strategies we personally designed to keep us safely in our comfort zones.

Unfortunately, those constructed comfort zones can hold us back from realizing our potential.

* * * * *

I had a friend who started several business ventures, but as soon as they became successful, she would go out of business. Years later, she realized her complicated relationship with money. She had grown up in a home with very little. Her father struggled to make ends meet and there were constant derogatory references to "those rich people" and the evil things people did with money. She knew from childhood that she was not like "those people" and as such, continued to sabotage her endeavors every time she made enough money that she didn't have to struggle any more.

Once she figured it out and she could consciously make more effective choices and she turned her financial situation around.

Physiological and Emotional Symptoms

When we get close to the edge of our comfort zone, there are discernible physiological effects. These are the symptoms of stress, created by our bodies in fight or flight mode. Have you ever felt your heart rate increase when you were under stress, felt your hands get cold or clammy or your face become flushed? These are the same universal symptoms that we discussed in the previous chapter. We cannot avoid, escape or quash these symptoms. We cannot out run or out smart them. They are our body's way of warning us that we are about to leave the "Known Zone." Remember to BREATHE!

But, while we may not be able to outrun these symptoms, we can learn to tame them by identifying and naming them. We can learn to pay attention to when and why we get the metaphorical "zap" from the electrical fences we've built over time, learn their location and origins, and methodically, intentionally, unearth the wires, move them, and *stretch* our comfort zones.

There are also emotional results when we near the edge of our comfort zone.

We may become angry, withdrawn, scared, or sad. Some of us may use humor to relieve the tension. Intellectually we respond with excuses and reasons why we can't, won't, or shouldn't do something if it is outside our comfort zone.

These protective barriers become our prisons over time. Our patterned responses go to work to help us deal with the discomfort. They kick in at unwanted moments. We don't think about it; it just happens unconsciously until it becomes a pattern.

Some of us have built iron fences in our lives that hold us captive and prevent us from achieving the things we desperately want, but are afraid to venture out to claim. If you could break free of your comfort zone, think of what you might discover, accomplish, become. What's waiting for you outside your self-imposed fences?

These are your dreams, your hopes and goals.

This is not to say that being comfortable is a bad thing. There is nothing wrong with feeling safe. It only becomes an issue when we make staying safe (comfortable) an excuse for complaining or the reason for our lack of fulfillment.

We can't have it both ways. We can dream of an omelet, but that dream will never become a reality unless we are willing to leave our comfort zone, head to the kitchen, and break a few eggs.

Two Ways to Motivate Yourself

Those who leave things until the last minute are using the bottom of their comfort zone to motivate themselves. That's called **procrastination.** If you have ever stayed up all night writing a paper or finishing a project, then you know what I mean. This method of motivation ("I work best under pressure"), may be effective in the short term, but proves exhausting over time and threatens your ability to develop resilience.

There is a less stressful and a less costly motivation than using fear, and that is to stay focused on what we *want*, long term, and to make proactive choices, rather than reactive ones.

To do that, we must know *why* it's important to us and, more importantly, be willing to step out into the unknown to create it.

The only thing that will get us beyond the discomfort of our fear-based boundaries, all those underground electric wires we've forgotten we buried, is a very clear sense of **what we want and why it's important to us.** Knowing and holding tight to our purpose is the only way to break through the top of our comfort zone.

The larger your comfort zone, the more confident you become.

Wrapping it Up

Our various comfort zones serve to either help or hinder our growth. Recognizing the initial warning signals (feelings of nervousness, frustration, or guilt, for example) and reflecting with curiosity about why we're feeling what we're feeling, allows us to identify and move beyond our unconscious constraints, often self-imposed.

Feeling comfortable is something we all enjoy. But if it comes at the cost of our hopes and dreams and desires for a better future–if we relinquish them and complain about the way things are because we're scared of changing–then staying comfortable becomes soul-deadening.

As leaders, it's important to understand ourselves before we ask others to follow us.

You cannot teach what you do not know.
You cannot lead where you will not go.

Making it Stick

Answer the following questions:

- In what kinds of situations do you typically hit the bottom of your comfort zone?

- In what kinds of situations do you typically hit the top of your comfort zone?

- What is your purpose, the driver that can help you push past the barriers of your comfort zone and take a risk in those situations?

- In times when you have pushed outside of your comfort zone, how well did you rebound and grow?

Taking It with You

- Our comfort zone keeps us trapped at both the top and bottom, clogging our potential and slowing our progress.

- The only way to break out of the top of our comfort zone is to know what we want and why it is important to us. Determine your purpose and hold tightly to it.

- Putting a support system in place to help us get there is the only way to get where we want to go. No one succeeds or claims their dreams without the assistance of others.

CHAPTER 5

Derailers Of A Resilient Mindset: Guilt And Resentment: The Cancers That Eat Resilience Alive

"Guilt is a cancer."

– David Grohl

The ability to let go of guilt and resentment can impact our progress towards resilience more than any other idea presented in this book. Many participants in our programs have shared that sentiment. This ability impacts our attitudes and if we don't get a handle on these emotions, they threaten to de-rail us from building resilience.

What do we do when guilt or resentment hijack an effective attitude for us? It's almost impossible to be an engaged, productive person when **guilt** or **resentment** has become our constant companion.

Guilt and resentment are core emotions we all experience, but they can be toxic when they drive the image that we present to the world. They are also the two attitudes that *undermine* our effectiveness most often, regardless of how or where we hide them. It's that pesky human nature thing again. Guilt, resentment, and frustration are all siblings of anger.

Here is a bit of context to introduce a potentially confrontational notion:

We're not encouraged to say the word "anger" in corporate circles. We can say we're "frustrated" or "annoyed" or "upset" or "irritated" or that we're "experiencing push-back," but it's taboo to utter the "A" word. Heaven help us, if we verbally slip, someone might send us off to HR for anger management class. And we know how well that works!

Frustration is the most commonly used word to describe any anger experienced inwardly or outwardly. Guilt, resentment, and frustration are all ways to describe being angry. We can think of guilt as anger with the self, and resentment as anger directed toward another person (or group of persons).

Guilt = Anger with the self–an internal focus
Resentment = Anger with someone else–an external focus

We Have Many Masks

We all hold certain images of ourselves. And we hold images of others, too, largely influenced by our filters, how we were raised, our experiences, etc. When we disappoint ourselves (or someone else) or when someone else disappoints us, we may respond (at least internally) with a sense of frustration, based on a fear we have that threatens our identity. This may not be visible to other people, but we feel it *inside.*

Many a person has stomped off to the washroom to hide in a stall after a crushing conversation. It's estimated that 70% of us have shed a tear or two at work.

Emotions show up everywhere.

$$* \quad * \quad * \quad * \quad *$$

Maria is an HR Director who had prepared for days to lead a difficult employee meeting in a factory. The discussion was heated because the difficult news she was delivering affected people's jobs and the amount of time off they would receive over the holidays.

During the meeting she lost control of the room. People yelled and demanded answers. They bullied her and derailed the agenda while she valiantly tried to sincerely address their concerns.

These employees were justified in their feelings because the situation had impacted them deeply. Through it all, Maria never lost her cool and, to her credit, handled the situation well.

The next day, however, she was overcome with deep anger at the people in the meeting. This emotion felt irrational to her because she knew they were justified, and their reaction had not been entirely inappropriate or unexpected. She also knew they were not angry at her, personally, but at the organization she represented.

Maria took some time to process the situation and determined she was angry because she stood to lose the good relationship with the employees she had always prided herself on having. She realized she would now have to rebuild credibility when it was not her fault that she had lost it in the first place.

Ultimately, under all the negative feelings, anger of any kind boils down to FEAR–the fear of losing something important and fundamental to ourselves, like our identities, our self-images.

When we're angry, figuring out what we might be afraid of is a great way to start the process of resolving the anger. Most likely it is a fear of what we stand to lose, especially a piece of our precious image. Truth has a way of cutting to the core. Keep looking until you get to the core of your fear. Only then can you do something about it.

Fear can present itself in a myriad of ways. It may feel like anxiety, frustration, trepidation, guilt or just plain anger.

- When we are angry or frustrated with ourselves (fear inside), it manifests as guilt or shame

- When we are angry or frustrated with others (fear outside), it manifests as resentment or blame

Guilt, shame, resentment and blame tend to work together creating a downward spiral that breeds toxic work environments. An effective first step to building organizational resilience is to start conversations that make it safe to discuss, acknowledge and work through these.

Have you ever felt guilty for resenting someone, or felt resentful after feeling guilty? These feelings tend to go hand-in-hand; we often bounce back and forth between them.

It is tough to get through difficult situations with these kinds of feelings when we are a member of a team, much less come back *stronger* from them. There is no way we can do our best work when we are caught in guilt, shame, resentment or fear.

Getting Out of Guilt & Resentment

As mentioned earlier, we each have two images: The image we hold of ourselves, and the one we project to the world.

The image we hold of ourselves represents who we *think* we are, seasoned with a sprinkle of who we want to become.

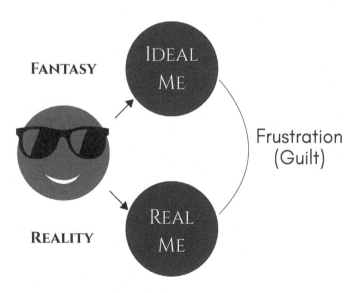

The Fantasy of Guilt

The **"real me"** in the diagram to the right, represents who we are, plain and simple, without the whitewash. The "ideal me" is a fantasy. It may be what we *want*, or the standard we hold for ourselves, but it isn't real–not yet, anyway.

The *real me* is, well, reality: What I do, what I say, my results. We only experience guilt when there is a gap between who we think we *should* be–the "ideal me," the fantasy, the person who *never* makes a mistake or falls short–and who we really are based on what we just did or said.

Guilt is the feeling that bridges that gap. Contrary to popular belief, guilt doesn't motivate us to change. It actually promotes self-protection.

And just as we hold images of ourselves, we also hold them of others, and who we think they *should* be and how they *should* behave.

The image we hold of others (the "ideal you") represents who we want or expect the other person to be, whether they know it or not. The "ideal you" is about who they are in our minds, our fantasy of them.

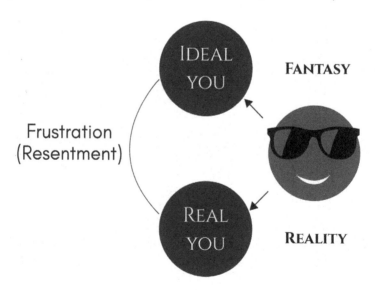

The Fantasy of Frustration

The "real you" represents who the other person is, based on what they do and say. We feel resentment when who they really are does not match who we believe they *should* be.

Resentment is the feeling that bridges *that* gap. It's also a protection mechanism.

As Maya Angelou said, "when people show you who they really are, believe them."

Here's the bottom-line:

Guilt and Resentment are flashing red lights that we are caught in a fantasy!

Take a moment to absorb that.

When we experience guilt, we are struggling to protect an image that *isn't real*. We just want it to be real. We are, in fact, in that moment, fooling ourselves, trying to keep a piece of our *imaginary* image intact. When we resent someone, we are attempting to protect the imaginary image we have of them.

"And there's this guy you'll need to fire," my new boss said, complaining that this employee used to be great, but wasn't getting his job done. As I took notes on my first day at a new job, my boss went on to say that this employee and his wife BOTH had stage four cancer. "If we let him go now, we won't have to pay all these benefits. Just find a way to get rid of him so we don't have to pay any severance."

I was as angry as I've ever been, furious, in fact. What kind of company does that? Who did my boss think she was? I thought I had joined a company with a great brand and reputation. I resented them for how they dared treat an employee with nearly thirty years of loyalty.

*Taking stock of my options, it became clear to me that despite my best intentions, I had joined an organization that **was** cut-throat enough to fire a guy with cancer instead of severing him as part of a reorganization that was in progress.*

I had a choice to make.

We always have choice.

As long as I chose to believe this wasn't that kind of company, I could live in denial and eventually he would be fired, if not by me then by someone else. My other option was to acknowledge that I had made an inaccurate assessment of this company and attempt do something about it.

I spent three months figuring out how to get approval for a rightful severance package for the employee in question. He deserved to be taken care of the way he took care of his team for over a quarter of a century. The day the ink on that package was signed, I exercised my choice to get out of a place I had misjudged from the start.

Facing the reality of who they were and choosing to leave was a lot healthier than the stress of staying angry at the corporation for not being the way I thought they should be. No amount of resentment on my part would change them – it would only change me.

Guilt denies reality to save us the pain of changing.

Many of us hold unrealistic images of what a "good person" is or does. Our differing backgrounds and cultures complicate this, but everyone was raised with certain expectations of what a good mother or good father or spouse was or should have been.

We come to the office with widely different expectations of what it means to be a good manager, a good leader, a good employee or a good co-worker. We confuse "good" with "perfect" and make our expectations so huge, so unattainable, no one, including ourselves, can possibly live up to them. As a result, many of us use guilt to manage perceived shortcomings that never end.

Guilt whispers in our ear, "I know I'm doing that, but it's not really me." As long as we feel guilty (If you weren't a "good" person you wouldn't feel guilty, right?), we get to avoid confronting ourselves. We don't have to tell ourselves the *truth*. Because once we do, we are faced with a choice. And it is with this choice that we can now change our reality.

Tell Yourself the Truth

There is only one way out of guilt: *Acknowledge the current reality and do something about it.*

When faced with current reality, one where we feel guilt, we are given a choice immediately: We can *change the image we're holding or change our guilt-inducing behavior.* Either choice ends the guilt, allowing us to move forward.

Resentment works the same way.

Resentment says: *"You're behaving the wrong way, so change!"* Resentment has a double payoff: It allows us to maintain our image of other people (who we think they ought to be) *and* we don't have to look at ourselves. *We* don't have to change, we can simply wait for *them* to change.

The reality is that resentment doesn't change a darn thing.

Many of us have, on occasion, resented a traffic jam that made us late to an appointment. When we get resentful, do people get out of the way? How about that feeling when someone takes credit for our idea in a meeting? Did resentment fix *that* situation?

Resentment, just like guilt, is a lousy motivator. When we revert to resentment, we divert our focus from our self–the only part of the equation we can control–to the other person or the situation. We relinquish control of the outcome. And we do so right in the moment when making an intentional choice is the most critical thing we can do.

It may not be fair. That makes no difference here. And it may be justified – we have a right to our feelings – but that doesn't matter either.

What does matter is that when we need to think clearly in difficult situations, **resentment undermines our ability to see, think, and behave in a clear and proactive fashion.**

Our next move is all about how long we choose to stay there.

Ask yourself:

- Is feeling guilty or resentful improving your performance?

- Do these two attitudes improve the quality of your life or the ability to come back more effectively from setbacks?

If your answers are "no" then know this: Frustration, annoyance, anxiety, guilt, resentment and shame are all variations of feeling angry, and anger is a smoke screen we put up to hide **FEAR.**

Anger is ALWAYS a reflection of FEAR.

Wrapping it Up

The next time we feel angry or resentful towards someone, it is helpful to stop for a moment and ask: "What might I be afraid of right now?" The answer will likely reflect a fear we have: Being unworthy, being exposed, not being good enough, losing a perception we pride ourselves on, etc. We may also be afraid that the other person is not who we hoped or thought they were.

Further complicating this is the fact that not only do we hold images of ourselves, but others hold images of us, too. All these images are the reason for Kegan's assertion that people are doing a second full-time job simply trying to manage people's perceptions. The more energy we expend managing our images (or hiding behind them), the less energy we have available to solve real problems or tackle opportunities, and the less energy we have for building resilience.

Trying to maintain an image of perfection is exhausting and ultimately destructive. And holding people to unrealistic standards sets us up for constant disappointment, perpetuating the cancers of guilt and resentment.

Making It Stick

1. Think of a situation where you felt guilty. In that moment of guilt:

    *   What part of your image were you trying to protect?

    *   Why was that important to you?

    *   What did you stand to lose?

    *   What was the reality about you in that situation that you could have chosen to face?

    *   What choice does that reality present?

Example: Mike felt guilty for missing his only son's soccer game when he had to work late to finish a project. This was important because Mike promised his son he would be there to see him kick his first goal. He felt guilty because to him, a "good father" does not break promises and goes to his son's games.

Mike's reality is that he did break a promise to his son. The sooner Mike realizes that he DID NOT live up to his image of a "good father," he can begin to resolve his guilt. He can apologize and make it up to his son and choose to do things differently in the future OR cut himself some slack because perfection may not be possible in this case. To do that, Mike would have to lose his image of himself as the perfect father.

Mike can also acknowledge that his image of a "good father" and a "good team player at work" will sometimes conflict. While it is realistic to think he can be both of those things, it is not realistic to think he can always be both at the same time.

Mike's ability to recognize that and make intentional choices about what to do in the moment will go a long way to help him move forward when things go awry in either role.

2. Think of a situation where you were angry with or resentful of someone at home. In that moment:

- Were there expectations you had of them that they were not living up to?

- What were you afraid of in that situation?

- What did you stand to lose?

- What was the reality you could have chosen to face to end the anger or resentment?

> *Example: Julie was angry. Her husband, Jim, constantly left his clothes wherever he took them off. On any given day, there were smelly socks and t-shirts littering the bedroom floor. Julie's expectation was that a "good husband," one that cared about her, would understand that she was not the maid.*
>
> *Julie was afraid that she would forever be picking up after Jim, but perhaps even more critical, her real fear (rational or not) was that if Jim didn't care enough about her to pick up his socks, maybe he really didn't care that much about her. She did not want to lose her otherwise happy marriage. Julie came to realize that Jim did assume that she would pick up his socks. She always did, so why should he assume differently?*
>
> *That left her with a choice; She could either continue picking up the socks or have a conversation with Jim about how she felt when he left them on the floor.*

3. Think of a situation where you were angry or resentful of a person or a situation at the office. In that moment:

- What might you have been afraid of?

- What did you stand to lose?

- What reality did you have to come to grips with in order to move past the situation?

Example: Ellie's boss, John, seemed to rev up the workload at the office right around 5:30 every afternoon.

John's kids were grown, his marriage was on the rocks, and he didn't really want to go home. Ellie, however, had two small children waiting for her at home and a nanny who by contract, needed to be relieved for the day.

Ellie resented the fact that her boss constantly scheduled meetings after 5:00 pm and made subtle comments to him about how late she was constantly forced to leave the office, although she always came in early every morning. But John wasn't getting the message.

Ellie had an expectation that a sensitive boss would understand her family obligations and the need for fairness in her work schedule. When she thought about it, she realized that she was afraid that her career might go sideways because John didn't respect her. She finally came to grips with the fact that John was not the kind of boss she thought he should be. She then had to make a choice about how to handle it.

Her options included putting up with it, talking to John and explaining her situation, talking to HR or looking for a new job.

Taking it With You

- When you are angry or frustrated with yourself (internalized fear), it manifests as guilt or shame.

- When you are angry or frustrated with others (externalized fear), it manifests as resentment or blame.

- Guilt and resentment are like flashing red lights that you are stuck in *fantasy*, perpetuating a world of unrealistic expectations.

- Guilt dissipates when you tell yourself the truth about your own behavior. Resentment dissipates when you tell yourself the truth about the person or situation you resent.

CHAPTER 6

Intentional Choices: How To Stop Chosing Without Thinking

Resilience IS A RESULT OF:

"In the power to change yourself lies the power to change the world around you."

– Anwar Sadat

President Anwar Sadat of Egypt was assassinated in 1981 by gunmen as he watched a military parade in Cairo. Sadat was a decisive leader who made choices based upon his passionate convictions.

He had led Egypt into the Yom Kippur War in 1973 in an attempt to regain the Sinai Peninsula from Israel, but his subsequent negotiation and agreement with Israel's Prime Minister, Menachim Begin, which culminated in the 1979 Egypt-Israel Peace Treaty, had angered extremist Muslims and had seen Egypt suspended from the Arab League.

Some choices cost us everything.

* * * * *

That choice, for Anwar Sadat, not only changed the world; it cost him his life.

Every one of us makes choices daily with far less at stake, but that doesn't minimize our need to make wise decisions. The choices we make define us, and the consequences linked to them vary in importance.

If we want to assess if something is working or not, there's only one place to look: the results we've created so far. Our results are the clearest indicator of the nature and effectiveness of the choices we've made in the past. One could say that our results are also the clearest indicator of what is most important to us.

Our results reflect the way we assimilate information (our filters) and the beliefs we hold about ourselves and others (images).

There are basically *three categories* for the kinds of choices we make every day:

- **Things we want to do:** *I want to go to the party*

- **Things we have to do:** *I have to take out the trash*

- **And, the things we do unconsciously:** *How did I get here?*

The things we want to do are easy choices. The things we feel we have to do, such as pay our taxes or go to the dentist, we sometimes do with a bit of annoyance or resentment.

Resilience IS A RESULT OF:

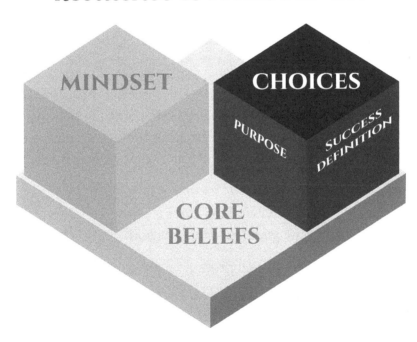

You are here: Purpose & Success Definition

And then there are the things we do *unconsciously*, things handled on our behalf, like breathing and blinking, reflexive responses.

But we often do other things unconsciously, too.

Have you ever been driving a car headed towards your new home or office, having just moved a few weeks ago, only to find yourself suddenly turning down the street towards your *old* home? How did that happen?

I'll tell you how. You were so busy thinking about something else – your conscious mind was so "off-line" – that your unconscious took over for you; it turned you toward a destination you'd driven to for years and knew well. Your unconscious mind made the choice for you because you weren't paying attention. It may feel as if there were no choice made at that moment, but at some level, there was a choice, because there you are, at your old house! It happens to all of us.

Our unconscious–and the choices it can and will make for us–are powerful things. Dancers and athletes talk about muscle memory. Once learned, skills return quickly because the unconscious *enables* progress, instead of *hindering* it. This is why paying attention is so important.

> *To make choices with* **intention,**
> *we must first pay* **attention.**

Our lives, both personally and professionally, and our organizations are the reflection of the sum of the choices we've made over time, and the choices we continue to make every day.

What choices have we made that get in the way of becoming our best and prevent us from bringing out the resilient warrior inside? These are the things we do, the ways we think or speak, and the ways we feel, that we judge as not working very well. These are things that get in the way of our being our best selves, or about which we feel lousy, or wish we would have done something differently.

Over time, these choices become **blockages**, stymieing our best efforts to get ahead.

In a corporate sense, what about your organization? What are some of the choices it makes that don't work out very well? What decisions get in the way of fully engaging all employees in delivering your objectives, strategy or mission (your business results)?

What are the things that happen that don't support or drive a culture that best serves your organization?

Blockages

Blockages are things we do and wish we didn't, or ways we sometimes feel that we wish we didn't, or ways we think, that we know are limiting. The problem isn't that we do/say/feel these ways, it's when we do/say/feel those things too much or too often, to our own detriment, so that it becomes a problem. Worse, we are aware of it, but don't know how to stop it because we are stuck in a comfort zone that doesn't serve us well in the situation.

In many of the leadership workshops the authors conduct, participants are asked to help make a list of potential blockages. Let me stress *potential* blockages, because in and of themselves, nothing on the list below is inherently good or bad, it's the way we use it that determines its effectiveness.

The choice to exercise is great, isn't it? Of course, it is, unless you're exercising at the gym every day to escape having a difficult conversation with your spouse or are overdoing it due to addiction. Likewise, a hammer may be an effective tool that can build a home and it can also be used as a murder weapon. It all depends on the *intention* of the user.

After almost three decades and hundreds of programs conducted at all levels in every culture and industry around the world, here is a summary of the kinds of things we capture on flip charts from leaders. Every. Time.

Blockages (in no particular order)

Behaviors:

Withdraw	Do housework	Eat
Get revenge	Phone someone	Take drugs
Sleep/watch TV	Work	Drink
Exercise	Complain	Quit
Read	Organize/socialize	

Attitude & Beliefs:

I'm too tired	It'll never work out	I don't deserve it
I don't have time	It's too late for me	I can't afford it
I'm right	It's their fault	I'm bored
I'll do it later	No one cares anyway	Why me?
I'm not smart enough	My.... won't approve	

Emotions:

Resentment	Frustration	Guilt
Melancholy	Fear	Anger
Bitterness	Depression	Hurt
Panic	Sadness	Jealousy
Hatred	Loneliness	

So, here's my question: If we can see this stuff isn't working for us, why do we keep *choosing* to do it?

Would we continue to invest in a stock year after year if it never produced a profit or a dividend financially? Of course not. So why do we keep investing, emotionally, in behaviors, thoughts and feelings that only seem to hurt ourselves?

We keep doing this stuff because we're getting a *payoff!*

We're not stupid, we're getting something out of it. If we can figure out what that payoff is, then we can try a better way to get the same payoff without paying the same prices.

Prices and Pay-Offs

Let's look at the relationship between these patterns of protection and their payoffs.

We make cost/benefit analyses internally and impulsively *before* we act, even if we are unaware of it, based largely (once again) on our filters. Even if unconsciously, we consider the costs and benefits for *everything* we do and think, and we are masters at rationalizing our choices.

Have you ever tried to justify a purchase or business decision and not really known why you made it? That's what addicts do, too. In most cases, we are looking for a **short-term** payoff, usually in the form of stress relief in the moment or an escape from the negative emotions associated with being near the edge of our comfort zones. This even shows up in our attempts to maximize our comfort and minimize the negative emotion in a difficult conversation with a spouse or direct report. It's human nature.

Think of the last time you "lost your cool." We usually have a good reason for doing so, even if we regret it afterwards. Maybe you even apologized. And, I bet that it will happen again, and you'll think it's about the situation or the other person.

But it isn't.

It's about *you* and your personal pay-off.

If companies (and even countries) make decisions based on analyses of their potential profit picture, so do we, though we may not be aware of the calculation taking place inside us. The trick is to figure out *consciously* what we're seeking *unconsciously*, so we can change it, before we sabotage our results.

Let's take the example of micro-managing.

Everybody hates this tedious "management" style. It undermines team morale, employee engagement, the leader's credibility, and blocks creative problem-solving and initiative. Why, then, do so many people micro-manage, not only at the office, but at home, on volunteer committees, in church groups and even dinner table discussions?

Because they're scared. That's almost always the reason. It just doesn't feel like fear. It feels like control or perfectionism, which we can rationalize.

So many of us are scared that we're not a "good enough" leader/parent/colleague/friend that our defense is to try harder and paddle faster to keep or regain our control.

It's a valid perspective that micro-managing can, sometimes, be effective. If I was having a critical surgery, I would want the surgeon opening me up to micro-manage the hell out of the process! But there is a balance to be achieved, as in *when, where and how much* pressure to apply to produce the most effective return in both the long and the short -term?

It is this skill of discernment–developed only from reflection and self-examination–that fosters choices which take people from being good leaders to resilient leaders.

The diagram below contains the most common, universal prices and pay-offs for micro-managing.

Ask yourself, what does the behavior cost *you*? What does it cost your team or family? And what do you get out of it? Those are the first questions to ask to determine *better* ways to get the same rewards.

BLOCKAGES

• Trust lowers
• Disengagement
• Resistence to change
• Team retention
• Lack innovation/collaboration
• Lack of leadership initiative
• Self-esteem
• Health - physical and emotional

COSTS

PAYOFFS

• Control (illusion of)
• Power
• Release
• Solitude
• Feel justified
• Get to be right
• Safety

Payoffs and Benefits

Look at that juicy pile of payoffs. Are any of these things wrong to want? No. Who doesn't want to feel powerful, in control and self-confident? All of us want that those things. The question is, how are we generating those emotional pay-offs, and at what cost to ourselves and those we lead and love?

Based on results, micromanagers want the experience of short-term control–and the price they pay is lowered team trust–more than they want an empowered team, which can only succeed if they give up some of their control and reach for the longer-term payoff.

When they finally *choose* to relinquish some control, they will not only see their employees improve performance, but also that the company reaches its potential.

> *"My belief is that if you're complaining about something for*
> *more than three minutes, two minutes ago*
> *you should have done something about it."*
>
> – Caitlin Moran

Another example of an ineffective behavior is complaining. Complaining is a common strategy people choose, unconsciously, in order to try and connect with others. If the weather is miserable and someone at the office comes in complaining about the cold, or snow, or rain, or wind, *somebody's* going to look up and agree with them. In the grocery store line when the elderly woman ahead of us pulls out her check book, the quickest way to make a connection is to roll our eyes at the guy in line behind us. The short-term pay-offs for complaining are rich: get attention, get to be right, get to connect. But long-term? Nobody likes hanging with a chronic complainer.

A Note on "Shoulds"

Saying (or thinking) we really "should" do something is a message to our unconscious that it's something we really don't *want* to do. Since we don't want to do it, and since our unconscious's primary purpose is to protect us and watch out for our well-being (which includes staying comfortable) our mind goes to work to help us avoid what we said we "should" do. Have you ever reminded yourself to do something in the morning, like call so-and-so, and then you go about your day, and when you get into bed that night and finally relax, your eyes fly open as you suddenly remember you forgot that one thing you reminded yourself you should do that same morning?

The problem with "shoulds" is that while we're consciously trying to underscore the importance of whatever it is we want to accomplish (I should take out the trash, I should go to the gym, etc.), we are actually undermining our efforts by coating our intentions with fear. (If I don't take out the trash, I'm a bad spouse, or my home will become a trash heap, etc., or whatever the negative consequence is.) *Shoulds* are a form of restrictive, punitive motivation. If you don't do/say/feel a certain way, it is easy to perceive yourself as a bad, flawed person. That's using guilt to motivate yourself and it rarely works in the long-term.

Welcome to one way in which we're making unconscious choices that undermine our effectiveness.

The way to help ourselves is to eliminate the word "should" from our minds. Replace it with "want" or, "could" which are less self-condemning concepts: "I want to call my mother today," or "I could go to the gym today."

Yes, it may feel like you're lying to yourself, short term, but longer-term, this one small substitution allows your unconscious to go to work to *help* your efforts, instead of *hindering* them. After only a few weeks, you will want to go to the gym based on the results you generate there. It will feel more like a comfortable choice made for a desired result, rather than a chore.

Also, how do you feel when someone tells you what you *should* do/say/feel? It usually brings out the warrior in me: "Oh, yeah? Make me!" That's hardly an enthusiastic agreement. But if someone says, "You could try (fill-in-the-blank) or, "You might want to consider..." then, I am more inclined to hear their input.

One last thing about the way you're "shoulding" all over yourself.

Remember: When we use that word about our self (or others) we reveal a certain belief we hold about what a perfect person would do/say/feel, all the time. How *unrealistic* is that? Back to that "ideal" image we want to maintain constantly or want others to maintain. It's a breeding ground for guilt and resentment. And so is "shoulding."

Just stop.

Wrapping it Up

Ineffective patterns of behavior are perpetuated by the payoffs they generate, often on an emotional level. While this is human nature, if we wish to increase our resilience and gain real control, it is important to understand the connection between the prices we pay for the payoffs we seek. Once we get back on the track of thinking through things with long-term goals in mind, we are more likely to make wiser, more proactive, intentional choices as a result.

When we go for short-term payoffs, we end up paying long-term prices. The trick is to flip that: Be willing to pay short-term prices for long-term pay-offs, emotionally, just as we do financially or physically. Why go to the gym or eat well? Because you're investing in your future. Let your team try something new. Resist the urge to check in with them, again. Trade the short-term discomfort for the longer-term pay-offs like increased team cohesion, lower turn-over, and improved trust.

Making it Stick

Pick a few blockages that you know get in the way for you. Use the list presented earlier in this chapter if you need help. Choose the things you do/think/say/feel most often that you know gets in your way and identify your costs and pay-offs from each.

Blockage	Cost of Doing It	Payoff for Doing It
Example: Cheating on my diet	*Sabotage results, self-respect, self-image, long-term satisfaction; fatigue*	*Immediate satisfaction, good taste, stress relief, short-term good feeling, avoid saying "no thank you"*

Taking It with You

- To be human is to make ineffective choices on occasion but if we do it *often* enough we create patterns that become blockages.

- Blockages are ways we think, things we say and do, and ways we feel that get in the way of effectiveness and resilience if used too often or too much.

- To change ineffective patterns of behavior, attitudes, or emotional responses, we must figure out what we're getting out of the particular pattern. What is our personal payoff? We wouldn't do it unless there *was* one, and a big one at that.

- Be willing to pay short-term prices for long term payoffs, just as we would with the stock market or a savings plan.

- We will probably be required to give up being right so often. Change only comes when we leave our comfort zones, like admitting when we've made a mistake.

- "Shoulds" *will* eventually cripple you. It is time to lose them. Either *choose* to do something, or *don't*, but don't "should" yourself into compliance. It's exhausting and hard on us and everyone around us.

CHAPTER 7:

Choices That Banish Change Fatigue Forever

Resilience IS A RESULT OF:

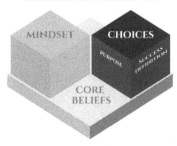

"Between stimulus and response, there is a space.
In that space is our power to choose our response.
In our response lies our growth and our freedom."

– Victor Frankl

It was the kind of professional coaching project that I had learned to turn down. A corporate Vice President asked me if I would make an exception with a troublesome employee named Judy. In all honesty, Judy should have been fired years ago. She was on her third performance improvement plan by the time she was assigned to me. I agreed to do her boss a favor and see if I could help her out.

Judy worked in HR where the need to handle difficult situations comes with the territory. But she was a bull in a china shop. A co-worker, Mark, came along, said something to set her off, and she snapped. The legal department got involved, an investigation was done, and I found myself talking to Judy about pushing the pause button before she launched her temper into orbit.

In the heat of the moment, when conversations escalate, and emotions run high, Judy just couldn't control that temper. As she told her side of the story to the attorney, she angrily announced, "It was Mark's fault!" because he had been inappropriate and angry. That was her defense. She denied the fact that she had let the situation between them escalate and she insisted, "I never raised my voice, I'm not that kind of person!" as she raised her voice defending herself.

The challenge I had was to help Judy to make intentional choices in the heat of the moment to be personally responsible for her rising anger and learn to "Push Pause."

Let's talk now about making more conscious, effective choices on a daily basis, the kind with long-term payoffs, because without that framework for participation in life, true effectiveness, and resilience, will remain out of reach. All the intellectual information in the world will not create more effective decision-making. Emotional intelligence, however, is so important to successful leadership that it helps off-set change fatigue in organizations and a victim mindset in individuals.

Consider the model below.

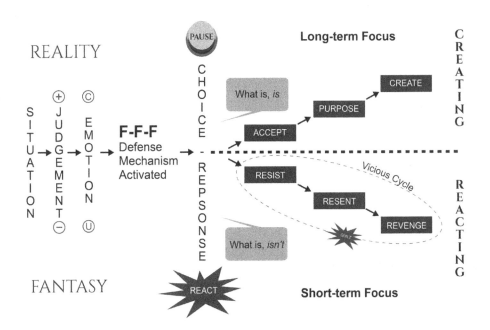

Taking Responsibility

Let's say a situation develops, maybe a misunderstanding with a co-worker. So, we go out and do something about it, perhaps send the person a text requesting to meet the following day, or maybe we gather our thoughts and write them in an email. Then, when we meet with this person, words are exchanged (a situation happens), and we are either pleased or disappointed by the outcome of that interchange and from that we form a judgement, either positive or negative.

That judgment triggers an emotion, either consciously or unconsciously, and maybe even our amygdala, and we are once again at moment of choice. We either make a *proactive* choice, consciously, pushing our proverbial pause button, or a *reactive* one, unconsciously. That brings us to the middle of the diagram.

Hit the Pause Button

Basically, this model suggests an *alternative* way to look at how we respond to situations, particularly when we are under stress.

Pausing during an emotional response buys us the time to be **intentional** about how we respond. It equips us to acknowledge what's really happening, face the facts and intentionally choose a response. Pushing the "pause button" and taking a deep breath, allows us to steer towards more intentional, proactive, long-term choices (above the line on the right side of the model).

Essentially, when a situation happens, in the blink of an eye we form a judgment. Based on, guess what? Your filters again. The judgment prompts an emotion or feeling (whether we realize it or not) which triggers a defense mechanism. From there, what we do is make a *choice*, even if it sometimes doesn't feel like it, just as driving to your old house didn't feel like a choice.

Let's say we head to Las Vegas on one day and manage to win a million bucks. We would most likely be giddy with excitement. We would have no problem accepting all the choices we made that produced this result because we are ecstatic about the result those choices created. We just won a million bucks! We would have no problem accepting that reality. We might even think, "The way it is, is fine by me!"

People don't resist change. They resist loss.

But what if we had *lost* a million dollars? We'd be bummed out, to say the least, and we might want to resist that result. We might want to wish it away because it was certainly *not* what we wanted or intended to do. We had intended to *win*. So, we resist the reality of it, maybe even saying, "The way it is, sucks!" or, "the way it is, shouldn't be."

At this point, we have entered *La La Land*: A fantasy built on the way it should've, could've or would've been, if only.

You are powerless when stuck in *La La Land*.

Or another example: Let's say we get dumped in a relationship or fired from our job. Chances are, we'd be a bit upset and resent the situation. Once we start resisting an outcome, it's usually a short slide from there into resentment.

And when we get a good case of resentment going, what's the logical next stage in this horrible cycle that keeps us locked in self-defeating patterns?

Revenge

Of course, we want to get even. That's what revenge is all about: notice the word, "even" is even in the word.

We all get revenge in a myriad of ways—subtle ways, aggressive ways, sly ways and unconscious ways. Have you ever called in sick when you weren't? Have you ever deliberately slowed down on the highway to block the driver tailgating behind you? Have you ever said something you knew would hurt someone else, but said it *anyway?* Sometimes even as the words leave our lips, we think, "No! Come back!" but by then it is too late, of course. Something in the moment takes hold of us. Even if we don't think *we* do these crazy things, we can probably all admit that we know someone who *does.* Welcome to passive-aggressive behaviors. Welcome to blockages that totally derail relationships and side-line professional advancement.

Welcome to the world of revenge. We have officially left the planet of personal responsibility.

Going below the line in the diagram above is to get stuck on the hamster wheel of the resist-resent-revenge cycle. It is ultimately destructive, but it allows us to hang on to being right about how wrong it all turned out. It's a bundle of juicy pay-offs.

Revenge is Completely at Odds with Resilience

If we want to build resilient organizations, we need to have serious conversations about our personal irresponsible issues and accountability, acknowledge the undertow of revenge, and equip people to get back above the line where they can face reality, and from there make sustainable and healthy decisions.

But, let's be honest, getting even also feels pretty good—great even—at least, at first. No matter how large or small the act of revenge, there's a little flash of pleasure.

In most cases, it is followed by the guilt hangover. "I shouldn't have done/said/felt that way. I should be better than this."

Yeah, so now we need to get "even" with ourselves. And how do we do that? In lots of unhealthy ways: We overeat, overspend, over drink, under rest, under exercise, take drugs, etc. We fall into an angst of self-punishment and deny ourselves the satisfaction and quality of life we truly want and need. It's like a slow death by a thousand cuts. They may be unconscious, but they still bleed fulfillment.

Remember the notion of authenticity and Kegan's research on how much time people spend managing their image? Well, the number one way we get revenge with *ourselves* is to hide behind our image and make what others think about us more important than the way we feel about ourselves.

The primary way we get revenge with *others* is to withdraw, to disengage emotionally. "My body's here, but my spirit has left the building." This applies to spousal, familial and work relationships as well. Have you ever worked in an office with people who "work together" but refuse to talk with each other? I hope not, but it's surprisingly common. Some families are like that, too.

We get really creative when we go into revenge mode. We use a lot of energy operating below the line, repeating old patterns of behavior, managing our image, keeping score, creating blame games, trading short-term pops of pleasure for long-term loss of confidence and clarity.

Being frightened or angry most of the time (or plotting little things that will annoy someone) is a lousy way to live. What's even more destructive is that we often don't even *realize* we're doing it.

Let's say something happens that we judge as negative (new boss, reorg, etc.) and our natural tendency is to go below the line and start complaining about the forthcoming event. We're exhibiting resistance, the *first* stage. If we do that for a little while, we'll be in resentment soon. It happens quickly.

So, knowing about payoffs now, and wanting to make more productive, creative choices, what could we choose? How do we go above the line in the face of a difficult, painful, or horrible situation? What could be powerful enough to lift us above the line, away from the juicy seduction of revenge, and assist us to accept a result we don't like, didn't ask for, and don't want?

The answer is straightforward. Just like beating an addiction, we must over-ride the natural human tendency to head below the line with an alternative fuel source: *Knowing our purpose.*

Staying above the line promotes strength, discipline, and a solution focus.

When we know our purpose in a situation, we will take the same energy we wasted being angry or resentful at someone or thing and choose instead to focus on creating what we're now clear is *more* important to us. That kind of clarity propels proactive choices. This is also what enables us to break the barrier of our comfort zone.

However, we're not talking about our life's purpose, although some of us may have already articulated one; this is about a **situational** purpose. The power of a clear situational purpose helps keep us on track and acts as a compass for consciously chosen, clearly understood decisions designed to create long-term, sustained change.

Above the line, we're creating. Below the line, we're reacting. Notice that the two words contain the same letters, rearranged.

While making conscious choices, staying above the line, and pressing the pause button are things leaders do consciously, resilient organizations can do these things too. It is easy to get defensive, and organizations are made up of people, so spiraling into revenge in a board room is easy. Yet there are stories of crisis where organizations paused to remember their purpose and values and made intentional choices about who they wanted to "be" in the moment of truth. In 1982, decisions made by Johnson & Johnson in the face of cyanide-laced Tylenol capsules cemented their reputation for keeping consumers safe. In the years since, companies like Toyota, Cadbury, Jet Blue, Starbucks and more have faced brand-threatening crises and leveraged those to build credibility by sticking to their purpose, values and principles.

Wrapping it Up

We all have the ability to choose our responses and to go *above* the line. It's the more difficult choice, at least short-term (because it takes more awareness and effort) but it produces long-term results that reflect internal alignment of values and priorities.

It also breeds self-respect and confidence. And, it invites respect from others, too. Once we gain clarity about our "whys" and start taking steps to stay above the line in difficult situations, we also gain the energy required to carry through on challenging initiatives.

Choices that suck you below the line are shallow short-term fixes. Above the line choices build long-term benefits.

Using the table on the next page

Making it Stick

- Recall a personal interaction, during which you now realize you went (and maybe stayed?) below the line, making the other person(s) or situation responsible for the outcome (i.e. your resentment). What were your personal payoffs? **Determine an alternative above-the-line choice you could have made.**

- Recall a professional interaction (at work), during which you now realize you went (and maybe stayed?) below the line, making the other person(s) or situation responsible for the outcome (i.e. your resentment). What were your personal payoffs? **Determine an alternative above-the-line choice you could have made.**

Interaction	Outcome	Payoffs	Alternative	Potential New Outcome
Example: A young woman ends a relationship. Her ex begins another relationship with a friend hers. He doesn't really like her so much as he knows it will upset his ex.	She is indeed upset. This now causes friends to "take sides," something the young man had not considered.	Short term gain: Sense of power, get to get even, don't have to look at reasons for the break-up. Long-term cost: Loss of friends, respect, trust, self-respect	Young man takes time after being hurt to examine how he contributed to the break-up, albeit potentially unwillingly. He doesn't date for several months.	He emerges from his pain a stronger, clearer young man, able to make thoughtful choices on whom he'll date.
Personal				

Interaction	Outcome	Payoffs	Alternative	Potential New Outcome
Example: Having been embarrassed in a meeting, EVP calls a client and bad-mouths (in an oblique way) the offending employee.	Client tells colleague, resulting in loss of trust and collaboration, as well as damaged client relations.	Short-term gain: sense of power/control, get to be right, don't have to look at self Long-term cost: trust reduced, damaged reputation, loss of integrity	EVP notices his internal reaction and examines his intention before asking to speak to the colleague directly. His colleague is important to the team and he wants to build for the future. He doesn't call the client.	Colleague is now aware of his offending behavior, EVP increases trust and models effective leadership

Professional

Taking it With You

- Making intentional choices requires learning to hit the pause button in emotionally charged moments: Take a deep breath—then respond.

- Resisting a reality we don't like thrusts us below the line into a fantasy world of "shoulds" in which we are powerless to respond proactively.

- To garner larger long-term pay-offs, we must be willing to pay smaller short-term costs, like giving up being right about the way it should be.

- Know your true purpose going into a situation. If it's to learn and connect you'll probably be fine. If it's to be right and impress, probably not.

- There is no room for revenge in a truly resilient person—or a truly resilient organization.

CHAPTER 8

Know Your Purpose: The Best Preparation For Rapid, Disruptive Change

Resilience IS A RESULT OF:

"Purpose derives from the question of why we do what we do. A good antidote is simply to ask "Why?""

– Juan Carlos Eichholz

I had taken over leading the Learning Function for a large retail company and Mark was part of the existing team. I knew little about him, but it was obvious he was a hard worker. He was personable, enthusiastic, and most often the first to arrive in the office every morning and the last to leave. Mark's job was to write training courses. He wrote facilitator guides for technical classes required by the "field." We had deadlines to deliver new courses and in the first month I was there, Mark missed his deadline.

With all the confidence of a new boss who thought she knew a thing or two about leadership, I went to Mark and asked him how long it would take for him to deliver his work the following month. I thought he would be more apt to deliver if he set his own timeline, so I invited Mark to set his own deadlines and was pretty sure we had a solution to the problem.

Another month went by and much to my surprise, Mark missed another deadline. So, I pulled out Plan C and installed a shiny new white board in the conference room. Every team member's projects and due dates were clearly listed for everyone to see. My hope was that the team would hold each other accountable. When Mark missed another deadline, I realized we had a more serious problem.

Mark continued to come in early and leave late but we had angry store managers who weren't getting the training they needed, and I was getting pressure to put Mark on a Performance Improvement Plan (PIP). I thought long and hard before I met with him. My purpose was clear: I wanted to find out what was going on. I vowed to try my best *to understand where he stood and not show my own frustration or reprimand him until I did.*

I started by explaining the position I was in and how my credibility was jeopardized when we missed deadlines, and how these missed deadlines had put our team in a bad spot. I could see him working hard but could not reconcile that with what he was delivering. Worse yet, I explained that I was going to be forced to put him on a PIP, the last step before termination. Then I asked him what his thoughts were. And I stopped talking.

At first, Mark quietly looked at his shoes. I waited. He slowly lifted his head. In a whisper, he mumbled, "I can't type." Mark was attempting to type 80-100 pages at a time using two fingers, the old 'hunt and peck' method. He was embarrassed to admit it, but a $15 typing tutorial solved this problem.

Had I'd gotten angry or he hadn't felt safe, I likely would have never understood the real issue. It was only having a clear purpose that saved the relationship and the employee.

"Efforts and courage are not enough without purpose and direction."

– John F. Kennedy

As an avid outdoor kid, one of the first things I remember asking for at Christmas was a good multi-purpose tool. Back then it was a Swiss Army knife called the *Huntsman.* It had two knives, a little saw, a scissors, can opener, screw driver, and about twenty other things on it for any possible emergency. It even had a toothpick and tweezers. I used it constantly for everything. Still do.

Our purpose is a lot like that.

It is invaluable to have a secret multi-purpose tool in our back pocket to help us stay on track, solve problems and get out of our comfort zone. Knowing our purpose requires us to understand our triggers and the emotions they spark—and helps us stay focused when they do. Awareness equips us to "press the pause button" before reacting automatically, and before the triggers hijack our best intentions.

Resilience IS A RESULT OF:

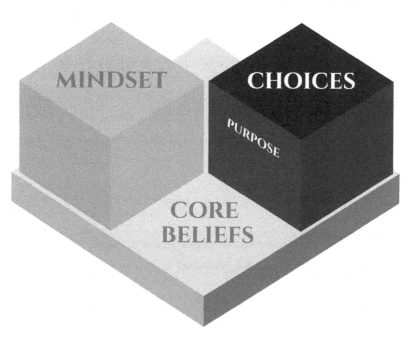

You are here: Purpose

When we "press pause," even just to take a breath, we buy time to assess the situation, seek advice and get clearer on our broader intentions. Clarity around our intentions allows us to choose a reaction that is *appropriate for the situation*. In life, while this may be difficult, it is necessary to control our responses. Companies do it every day when they plan to react to market fluctuations and competitive threats.

Your purpose is your highest and best intention in a situation.

The notion of purpose sometimes causes people to reflect on their over-arching purpose for their life, and while it certainly helps to have one, that is not exactly what we are referring to here. Purpose, in this context, is the highest and best desired outcome of the situation that is driving the need to *push pause.* The quality of the decision made in that moment, the capacity to be more resilient, is directly proportional to our ability to zero in on our purpose specific to the situation. Because that specific situation demands an immediate response.

Every situation gives us a chance to be who we really are.

Getting clear on your purpose is your little Swiss Army knife for your life.

Ideally, clarifying our purpose is the prework we need to complete before we open our mouths. It asks the critical question:

What is the single most important outcome I want from this interaction, or the leadership quality I need to demonstrate visibly in this situation?

Related to your team or those around you, "What is the most important message you want to convey to *others* involved in the situation?"

Think about your desired long-term outcomes. Ask yourself if this is a *pattern*, or if what you're dealing with is a one-time situation. When clarifying your purpose, often the most critical question to ask is:

If you could snap your fingers and change one thing about the other person (or group of people), what would it be?

To help think that through, we can ask what the stakes are for us—positive or negative–the business, the other party, the team, or anyone else involved. What stands to be lost or gained? We tend to focus on losses like losing a job, but often, there are greater stakes involved if you look at both positive and negative impacts for a broader group of stakeholders.

For example, if we have a team member who is not meeting deadlines, of course, they could be fired, but the reality is, we really don't want to do that and, most people know that's extreme. While it may seem most obvious, it may not be the stake that is most motivational in terms of creating behavioral change. Most people, however, do not come to work with the idea of hurting their boss or their team. If we think broader about the stakes and include losing our own credibility, there is a high likelihood that when someone realizes their actions are actually hurting their boss's credibility or the team's morale, they will begin to see the problem with missing deadlines.

Knowing the stakes helps clarify our situational purpose and enables us to create a dialog to solve issues with the highest and best outcome. Let's say a team leader has one employee who is chronically late to meetings. That person's tardiness is undermining the team's efforts, creating frustration and building resentment in those who are picking up the slack. It may also be costing productivity or risking their job. The upside of fixing it may be additional opportunities or problems solved.

Let's say the leader brings the employee in to talk to them to help them change their pattern, but the employee becomes defensive and resorts to verbal attacks, even accusing *the leader* of being a lousy manager. Sound a bit too familiar? Under the circumstances, as the boss who's trying to help that employee, it would be natural to become irritated, return the defensiveness, or raise one's voice. This is likely, not only to *not* solve the problem, but to shift the focus *away from* the real issue of tardiness, and into an unproductive argument of who is *right*.

What would it say to the team when the word got out (and it always does) that the boss reacted to the point of disrespecting a member of their team? It might get around that employees are not allowed to tell the boss what they think because the boss is dictatorial and inaccessible. That is not a perception we want to cultivate.

Instead of resorting to retaliatory tactics, the team leader could push the "pause button," take a deep breath, thank the employee for his or her feedback, and redirect the conversation back on point by stating,

> "I appreciate hearing your point of view, and it sounds like there's plenty there for a future conversation. Right now, we're talking about your tardiness. How can I support you to be on time?"

That would help send a message to the other team members that while firm, the boss will work with them, which is more in alignment with a long-term purpose to become a more effective leader.

Notice that the suggested response also defines a boundary, no deflections allowed—we're talking about *their* (the other party, in this case the employee) behavior here, not the boss's. Knowing our purpose allows us to make choices in alignment with a long-term goal. It's like putting on a pair of glasses we didn't even know we needed. Suddenly we can see things much more clearly.

Making it Stick

Situational Purpose Tool

Answer the questions below about a situation outside of work. Discuss the answers with someone else who can challenge you or push you on your thinking.

1. Recall a tough situation (or series of them) that you have been through where you wish you had been more effective in the moment and describe it briefly.

    _____

    _____

    _____

2. Think back to the situation. What was the one most important outcome?

    _____

    _____

    _____

3. Where, in the situation, could you have "pushed the pause button" and identified your purpose?

    _____

    _____

    _____

4. What kept you from doing that?

    _____

    _____

    _____

5. In this situation, what would you have liked your response to project about you?

    _____

    _____

    _____

6. Hypothetically, how could the outcome of the situation (the part you created) have been different if you had been clear on your purpose prior to forming your response?

    _____

    _____

    _____

Wrapping it Up

A clear purpose is your Swiss Army knife—a handy tool in tough spots. It acts as a compass when making choices. Making decisions is, by definition, a choice. Knowing our purpose allows us to make the most informed choice possible, right there in the moment, for the highest possible good. We can master this skill with consistent awareness and practice it in any situation, all day long.

Building resilience muscles in everyday situations when choices don't carry severe consequences is critical to having those muscles in shape and ready to be used when the chips are down and the consequences matter a lot.

Taking it With You

- Knowing our purpose requires us to be aware of what emotions get triggered in us and what those triggers are.

- Every situation is a chance to demonstrate to the world who we really are.

- To figure out your purpose, ask, *"What is the one most important outcome or attribute I need to demonstrate in this situation?"*

- Resilient people and organizations "push the pause button" and get clear on their purpose *before* they act.

- A clear purpose serves as the due north on your situational decision-making compass.

CHAPTER 9

Define Success:
Make The Right Choices
In The Heat Of Stress

Resilience IS A RESULT OF:

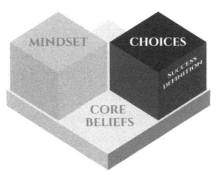

"Success is a journey, not a destination.
The doing is often more important than the outcome."

– Arthur Ashe

I realized my Honda Pilot was on fire just as the smoke began to turn black and the fumes filled the car. As flames shot out from underneath the steering wheel and black smoke engulfed the cabin, I somehow managed to steer out of traffic and into a parking lot, where, with one foot in a cast, I threw open the door, tossed my computer bag as far away as I could and followed it in a headfirst rolling dive away from the raging inferno.

For forty-five minutes, I stood in shock watching firefighters battle what they called, "one of the hottest fires they had ever seen," as I watched windows explode and my engine melt away to nothing. Standing there, I shuddered, realizing that had the fire started a mere thirty seconds later, I would have been on the ramp of a major interstate with little ability to pull off and survive the fire. Had there been children in car seats, there would not have been time to get them out.

When the car first ignited, I had just picked it up from being serviced and was on my way to meet a client. Following that meeting I planned to head out of town for a month. I had started packing so my car contained a lot of important stuff, all of which was lost. By the time the fire was out, the dealership service manager had arrived and laconically asked me, "What's next, Jennifer?"

"What's next" began in the office of the dealership's general manager. It was quickly determined that a service technician had spilled transmission fluid on the exhaust manifold and had neglected to clean it up. When the engine got hot, it ignited.

I was furious. This was a rookie mistake that almost cost me my life. But standing there watching the flames, I had complete clarity. The situation was largely out of my control. I had a strong value system based upon, "Impacting life with vigor instead of being happened to." I also knew that I could not afford to let the stress of the situation impact a health situation I had. All my fury, however justified, wasn't worth triggering another problem.

Guided by a clarity of purpose, I walked into the general manager's office knowing that I would not yell or be nasty. I would be reasonable, even if what had happened was unfair, and I would work to find a mutually acceptable resolution as quickly as possible.

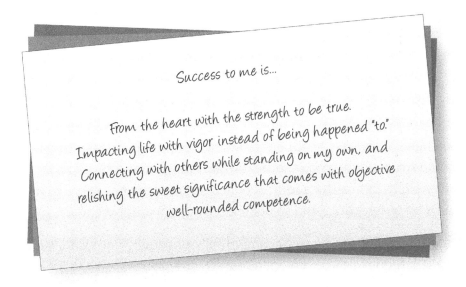

Jennifer's Definition of Success

I could have sued—I had a case and an incredible attorney—but the stress involved would not at all serve my immediate situational purpose, which was to get things back to normal as fast as possible and take back control of things.

Later, as I continued to process the trauma that had impacted my life in numerous ways, I realized how clarity around my definition of success had guided every decision I made in that situation, even in the face of distress and anger.

Surely, I could have come out better financially, but I made a conscious choice to trade money for decency, swiftness, staying true to my values, and the ability to get past it so I that could come back stronger, and faster.

It worked. And my near-death experience cemented my belief in having a definition of success.

"Define success on your own terms, achieve it by your own rules, and build a life you're proud to live."

– Anne Sweeney

You need a *compass* or a map (or at least a GPS) if you plan to take a journey from one place to another, or one "state" to another. To go from overweight to healthy and fit requires some planning, perseverance and a bit of direction. And so does surviving a fire, apparently.

To go from getting by to becoming fully engaged, from satisfied to fulfilled, requires some direction too.

Your Basic Emotional Needs

According to Maslow, human beings have a hierarchy of basic needs as reflected in the model seen here. While "self-actualization" may translate to profitable growth or achieving a mission, organizations have much the same hierarchy.

These **five basic needs are hierarchical** because we must have the first, and most basic, before we can focus on the next level. For example, it is difficult to think about connection to others when we are starving or to be worried about self-esteem during a war. First, we must BE safe and then we can FEEL safe.

SELF-ACTUALIZATION
Desire to be the most that one can be

ESTEEM
Respect, self-esteem, status, recognition, strength, freedom

LOVE AND BELONGING
Friendship, intimacy, family, sense of connection

SAFETY NEEDS
Personal security, employment, resources, health, property

PHYSIOLOGICAL NEEDS
Air, water, food, shelter, sleep, clothing, reproduction

Maslow's Hierarchy of Needs

When we feel physically, psychologically and emotionally safe, we bring the best versions of ourselves to our work and our relationships. It is only at that point that humans can *begin* to think about self-actualization, the land of character and integrity, the place where success is defined by self rather than systems.

Building our individual definition for success is a lot like a compass directing us to the internal experiences we require to feel alive. We must internalize it, memorizing it so that whether we are consciously aware or not, it is in the background, part of our default positioning, our perspective, constantly filtering out the junk that doesn't serve us, better equipping us to make instinctive in-the-moment choices that do serve us. Believe me when I tell you, it did not even occur to me that I had used it until months after I dove out of the flaming car.

It was through understanding how my definition of success had been ingrained in me enough to lead me to act in a way I was proud of, in the middle of a traumatic situation, that ended the trauma for good.

Your Unique Emotional Needs

Just as we have physical needs (like air, water, and rest), we each have emotional needs as well, experiences for which we long. When we don't know exactly what they are, we can end up going through life a little like a ball in a pinball machine, bouncing from one bumper to another, from one job or relationship to another, one policy or protocol to another, with little understanding of why, and not much control of our lives.

For example, some people aren't made for a nine-to-five job. Some of us have an emotional need for freedom or flexibility or autonomy that *supersedes* our need for security. But maybe we were told that we had to go that route anyway. Perhaps some of our parents valued security more highly than freedom. There are lots of reasons why our individual driving needs become obfuscated over time.

These emotional needs and the experiences that drive us, can be both required and highly desired. It's the difference between water and chocolate: we need water, we *want* chocolate. Our *required* emotional needs, when we haven't "fed" them for a while, can rear up, often hijacking our rational mind. If you've ever woken up one morning shaking your head about the night before, you were probably hijacked. For example, if we have a driving need for attention, and have felt marginalized or silenced in too many meetings, we might find ourselves suddenly blurting out something and regretting it. But we got everyone's attention; all eyes are on us now.

Further complicating things is the notion that once identified, we must learn how to feed our needs in a healthy way, *independent of other people.* That's important. Because if we wait for other people to provide us the opportunities to feel the ways we want to feel, we will wait a long time.

Let's say we have a driving need for admiration. We might strive for professional advancement, motivated by a desire for that experience, thinking that the only way we can feel admiration is to be admired by *others.* The idea here is to understand that we can feed these needs *internally.* Watching a beautiful sunset can evoke an internal sense of admiration, as can listening to beautiful music, or gazing at artistic creations. Dancing or cooking, or a hundred other things, could be our preferred choices of things to notice and admire. These rich experiences can feed our admiration need, intentionally, in a healthy, sustainable manner.

Once we learn how to identify our *unique, finite set* of emotional needs, then *we* drive our needs, they don't drive us. We find ways of creating experiences that fulfill them, constructively, rather than becoming a victim of those that don't. That's the true source of fulfillment we label "happy."

Fulfillment does not occur in the situation.
Fulfillment occurs in you.

We must be present and intentional to find it. Fulfillment is about how we make or find meaning in difficult situations and it is a critical characteristic – Coutu's second – of resilient people and organizations.

The Difference Between Happiness and Fulfillment

Lots of folks are looking to be happy. Everybody wants to be happy. But what exactly does that mean? And what's the difference between happiness and fulfillment?

When posed that question in a workshop once, a wise man compared it to different aspects of a piece of music: Happiness is the tune, while fulfillment is the base line, constantly keeping time, unifying the entire song.

Success in this context is about fulfillment. We might be happy to win the lottery in the short-term, but without fulfilling work of some kind, studies tell us we will wither away in the long term.

Getting clear on what success looks and feels like to us—who we're *being,* not only what we're doing—influences our ability to make more effective choices, both individually and organizationally. As we already know, childhood and work environment influences can obscure our own measuring sticks. It's a good idea to take stock of and recalibrate them every so often. That only happens if we pay attention and take some time for reflection.

Knowing how to measure success by your *own* standards, and not by those of other people, predetermines the success itself.

Your sense of fulfillment comes down to how you define success. And then, how you live it.

As you think through what success is to you, a good place to start is with your answers to these questions:

- When and where do you lose track of time?

- What are you doing at that moment?

- And what about that activity invites you to get lost in it (in a good way) while doing it?

For example: Some of us lose time when we are involved in artistic endeavors (music, art, calligraphy, and writing). While the mediums differ, the experience of accuracy and precision is common to them all.

Wrapping it Up

We have both physical and emotional needs. Some are required. We can hurt ourselves or those around us when we are unaware of what they are, or when they haven't been "fed" in a while.

Learning to identify and feed those needs in consciously chosen, constructive ways, to lead from a position of clarity and strength, improves resilience and promotes confidence.

Until we figure out what success means for us, we can often allow others to steer our ships toward shores that prove unfulfilling. Determining our individual emotional needs and consciously creating them assists in decision making.

A clearly defined purpose serves as an effective compass. It helps to know where we're headed when we set sail.

Making It Stick

Figure Out Your Driving Needs (You can do this for your organization too)

1. Make a list of 15 things you *want*. These can be things you want to do, places you want to go, things you want to own. Think big. Money is no object. Anything goes. The key is to make your list quickly, without self-censure. Then, give some thought to the actual experience you think you would have if you accomplished that item.

What I Want	Why I Want it– What Experience / Feeling
Example: *A cottage* *A reconditioned DeLorean*	*...to be in nature...to spend time with friends...etc. (Connection? Solitude? Achievement?)* *...freedom...achievement... elegance...uniqueness*

What I Want	Why I Want it— What Experience / Feeling

2. Now, make another list. This time, jot down at least **ten people you admire** on the left side. They can be someone you know personally or only know from a distance. They can be living or dead, real or fictional.

People I Admire	Characteristics I Admire In Them

People I Admire	Characteristics I Admire In Them

3. In the right column above, quickly, without much thought, jot down the characteristics of those people you listed above. Do you notice any overlap of traits?

   For example, if you admire four people for their loyalty, or compassion, chances are high you require those experiences in your life on an ongoing basis to feel fulfilled.

4. Now, on another sheet of paper, make one last list compiling the themes of the two lists above. You should end up with a list of about 7–10 words. Rank your top 3–5. These are most likely the *driving* needs of your life.

5. Create your personal definition of success by filling in the blanks of this sentence with the words you've culled:

   "Success to me means creating _____, _____, _____,

   and _____ consciously and proactively each day."

   • Read this every morning before you go to work. Post it on your bathroom mirror or your kitchen refrigerator.

   • Then, try doing it for your team, or company. When everyone has a clear picture of what success looks and feels like as a *team*, remarkable results can be achieved.

Taking it With You

- We were born with *emotional* needs as well as *physical* ones. Feeding those experiential needs in a healthy way is as important as feeding our bodies in a healthy way.

- Feeding our emotional needs consciously and constructively is the path to fulfillment.

- Once we have realized our unique driving needs, decision making becomes *streamlined.*

- Noticing when we come alive helps us understand our unique set of emotional requirements.

- Our purpose serves as a compass, and our finite list of driving needs serves as a map towards a fulfilling, successful life (or work environment) by our own standards.

CHAPTER 10

Core Beliefs: Know What You Stand On When You Need To Stand Up

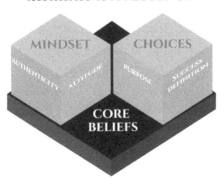

Resilience IS A RESULT OF:

*"Gandhi held no formal position of authority.
Nor was there an organized army standing behind him.
What he did have were his core beliefs."*

– Punit Renjen

Now to the final piece of the Leader*Shift*® Resilience Framework.

To review: Our resilience is determined by our mindset (authenticity and attitude) coupled with the choices we make (purpose and definition of success). They rest on the foundation of our *core beliefs,* or some might say, our faith. It's a question of what, or whom, we trust.

I need to ask a bit of forgiveness to talk about faith. I will talk about mine and challenge you to think about yours. It shocks people sometimes when faith comes up in a corporate workshop since it is a topic we are all taught to avoid at work. But faith is critical to resilience and great leadership. That's the shocking truth about faith in the workplace. It drives everything.

Everybody has faith in *something,* whether religious or otherwise.

It is important to note that faith, in this context, is very different from religion or our religious traditions and rituals. What we *do* is very different than what we *know.* I am talking about faith in terms of what we know.

Leadership, particularly in the adaptive context, is hard. It requires us to ask unpopular questions and to challenge the status quo. Sometimes we make unpopular decisions because we must for the greater good. Anyone who leads others gets stuck in difficult situations from time to time. This is what leaders sign up for when they step up to the challenge of influencing and guiding others. The willingness, ability and resilience to stand in those difficult situations day after day and come back for more are why we cannot all be great leaders. As I've studied leadership, one thing I've learned stands out:

It is difficult to stand up when you don't know
what you are standing on.

Our faith drives resilience and the choices we make by forming the basis of our ability to:

- Take risks and be authentic

- Choose our attitudes

- Let go of filters that don't serve us and select those that do

- Understand our purpose (for our life or a situation)

- Get clear on what success looks like

I had a boss who liked to say, "If you're not risking your career every day, you're risking your career." How (or why) in the world would anyone be willing to risk a career without the faith that either they are going to make the right decision every time, or that they are going to be okay when they really screw up? The bottom line is that to be effective, we need to take risks, and taking risks requires faith in *something*. The clearer we are about what that is for us, the more confident we will be.

That might mean faith in ourselves and our abilities, or it might mean faith that our boss has our back, or even that we are marketable enough to find another job if we need to. Perhaps it might mean that a higher power will guide us or take care of us when there's nowhere else to turn. These are all examples of core beliefs, the things or people in which we place our trust. For most of us, it is a bit of all of these, but here's what I know: I know *you've got to know what it is for you.* I say this because only knowing what is true for you will sustain you when it's all you've got. And maybe, just maybe, it's not the same for all of us.

So, this isn't about my faith or set of beliefs being "right" and trying to convince you that what I believe is true for *you.* And it's certainly not about how I choose to celebrate that faith. Throughout history, when just about any group has decided they have a monopoly on the truth, a war has broken out (think of the crusades, jihad, coups, dictatorships, etc.). That's not what I'm talking about here.

Think about this for a minute: We all have faith in something. But it's the reason people avoid the topic of "faith" at work like the plague. No one really likes to be *convinced* of anything. And, outside of Sunday morning, most folks don't benefit from being preached at. Often our traditions trump our beliefs, but if we know what we stand on, and what we stand for, we can be more confident to *stand up.* We can also be more open to the fact that others may have just as strong a "knowing" about something true for them.

Faith cannot be checked at the door to the office. It travels with us. It comes to work with us. We live it out loud each day. And so does everyone around us, whether we acknowledge it or not. It is important that we know what is true for us. That requires a bit of work. Many shy away from this because it tends to scratch at who we are, demanding answers to some tough questions, but if we are committed to building resilience, it is work we cannot avoid doing.

Sometimes the work of *knowing* our faith (what we trust in) requires letting go of the mantras we've been taught and rethinking what we really believe. This is not a time for recitation. It is a time to get real. It may not match our declared religion, culture of origin, or the verses we memorized as a kid. It may not agree with our family or friends.

Instead, it must reflect what we know, in the very core of our beings, to be true.

Give yourself permission to make that okay. We don't have to share it. We just need to wrestle it to the ground, so we know it and are clear and ready when we need to call it forth and rely on it or lean on it during the darker times.

It took a long time to get there, but I am certain of what I believe. I don't "believe" anymore. I *know.* I also know that this single fact is what has provided me the resilience I needed to thrive in face of over nine major life events in ten years. And I also know that "knowing" can help every one of us.

More directly, if you are a leader looking to build resilience, reduce stress and have more confidence to take risks and stand up in the face of all kinds of resistance, **you need to do the work to determine what is true for you**. You need to be able to understand and clearly articulate your faith, even if only for and to yourself.

Let me put it out there: I have a very strong faith in God. And I've done the work to figure out, for me, what kind of God that is. At this point, many of you have stopped reading. I realize that. My challenge to the rest of you is to hang with me a bit longer. I won't try to convert anyone to anything other than an understanding of why that kind of clarity is important, regardless of whether you believe in my God, Buddha, Mohammed, the universe, or your lucky rabbit foot key chain.

The point is that we all need to know without a shadow of a doubt what we believe, and why, and it needs to be strong and solid enough to support us when we need to step out on it all alone.

In 2009, my business failed. You may recall that no one was buying leadership workshops then. I had partnered with a company that was adamant that I not sell consulting, but instead focus on training. It was a hard lesson in meeting the market where they are and believe me, they were not into leadership development in the midst of a recession.

I made $1,000 that year (and no, that's not a typo). Thankfully, I had savings, but it wasn't enough. As I fought to reclaim my business, I hit the bottom of my checking account several times. During that same year, I was diagnosed with a life-altering illness.

Despite that, fear never entered my mind. This allowed me to make good decisions from a healthy place and negotiate from a point of strength when I finally had to go out of business and take a job offer. I knew, beyond doubt, that the God in whom I placed my trust would provide for me. And He did–repeatedly.

First it was an offer to buy my boat that was, to the dollar, the amount of a car repair I couldn't afford. Then, it was a lawsuit that was settled unexpectedly and kept me afloat for a few months. After that, it was a car I had had listed for months and miraculously, out of nowhere it sold for the asking price.

Every single time I hit rock bottom, God was there. When my God was all I had, He was all I needed. Because of my faith, I was able to thrive when all else failed.

It is easier to stand up when we know what we are standing on.

Let me be clear. I am not resilient because I came through a bunch of tough situations and thrived. Neither did Cynthia, who was an hour from death in 2005, and has her own tough times. No, we came through those situations and thrived *because* we were resilient. Because we know what we believed. Because we had built a strong foundation long before the stress hit, and that allowed us each to stop trying to control what we couldn't and focus on what we *could*. Building that kind of firm foundation is what makes up the Leader*Shift*® Resilience Framework, now proven effective with both individuals and organizations.

Organizationally, this work is even more challenging because it requires creating alignment from the bottom to the top levels. It also requires a healthy dose of what is real versus what is aspirational. An organization will never be resilient if its leaders align around a set of aspirational beliefs and values while ignoring the real—and perhaps unspoken—set of values that guides their decisions differently. Any work done to understand organizational beliefs must acknowledge and reconcile that dissonance.

When I was waterskiing competitively, I moved to Florida to train with one of the nation's elite slalom coaches, Chet Raley. At the time, I was young and arrogant and didn't think I needed help from anyone, much less a higher power. But, internally, I was floundering, falling apart inside. All my priorities were mixed up. If I'm honest, I was, "off the rails" and it was starting to show.

One morning, Chet and I got to the lake in time to watch the sunrise and as we sat on the steps of his equipment shed, he asked me, "Jennifer, do you believe in God?" When I said yes, he smiled and asked, "Do you believe, or do you know?"

*I muttered something about how you can never really know...faith is all about what we can't really know, right? Chet stopped. He looked me square in the eye and said, "I **know**."*

He was dead serious. He knew what was true for him beyond a shadow of a doubt.

*In an instant, I realized that I wanted that, too. I didn't have it, but I desperately **needed** it.*

We all do.

Chet was one of the smartest teachers and greatest mentors I've ever known. It has been over ten years since I've seen or spoken to him and not a day goes by that I don't think about what he taught me in a couple of months of water-ski training.

$$\ast \; \ast \; \ast \; \ast \; \ast$$

Knowing, beyond merely believing, means getting clear on what or who it is that you will hand the wheel to, when you know you cannot drive on your own strength.

What or who is it for *you?*

The foundation of resilience is knowing what you stand for.

Wrapping It Up

We must do the necessary internal work, personally, to be able to understand what we stand for long before we need it, and long before we need to manifest it externally during times of crisis or upheaval. That way, we can be sure that when everything around us is crashing, we can stand up because we know what we are standing **on.**

Some say that faith in ourselves is enough. But is there anyone who has never doubted themselves or the decisions they make when nothing seems to be going as expected? That's where God and faith come in.

Making it Stick

Think through the concepts below. Highlight those to which the answers do not come easy. Spend some time alone reflecting on them. It is not important what the answer is, as much as it is crucial for you to **know what is true** for you about the topic. This exercise makes some people uncomfortable, however often core beliefs are what separates resilient leaders from those who get stuck at the height of disruption. Think not just about what you believe or have been taught to think, but what one or two things do you really know for sure about:

A higher power	This life	What you need to do	Coincidences
Who has your back	Why you are here	Control	Truth
Who made you	Free will	Prayer	Your power
Where are you going	What guides you	The afterlife	Integrity
Your family	Ethics	Who or what you trust	Faith
Love	Your intuition	Divine will	How do you know
Your values	Your connection to spirituality	What true to yourself looks like	Where you turn when the chips are down

Taking It with You

- Our core beliefs are the foundation that underpins our ability to be resilient.

- Values spring from beliefs, and consciously known beliefs propel consciously chosen values in the form of daily, consistent choices.

- It is difficult to stand up in a difficult situation when we don't know what we are standing on, or if it will hold us.

- We are walking, talking reflections of our inner most beliefs. It would be wise to know what they are.

- Knowing what we believe *before* we need it, makes both us as individuals and our organizations more resilient in every moment.

PART TWO

Building Resilient Organizations

"The most resilient companies foster a pervasive culture of innovation at all levels of the organization - one that values risk-taking, embraces experimentation and considers failure an inevitable part of thinking boldly."

– Lynne Doughtie

CHAPTER 11

Becoming A Resilient Team

Resilience IS A RESULT OF:

"Difficulties break some men but make others."

– Nelson Mandela

L et us now turn our attention from becoming resilient leaders to building resilient organizations. We believe that resilience is the number one characteristic required for leaders today and almost no one is talking about it. If we are going to lead teams or organizations through the rapid changes that are rampant in in today's marketplace, we need to not only talk about it, we had better get good at it so we can build teams that are energized and elevated by disruption too.

Resilience: Who Needs It And Why?

As we seek to build resilient organizations, a question sometimes posed to us is, "Does everyone in the organization need to develop resilience?" The answer lies in the type of challenges people will be facing. It's difficult to imagine anyone who would not benefit from flexing and building resilience muscles, particularly in a leadership role of any kind, but the reality is that the degree to which people need resilience is somewhat proportional to the degree of adaptation required in the face of challenges and disruption. Those leading and mobilizing people to address adaptive challenges are likely to need more resilience that those in repetitive roles who are rarely disrupted. This book is focused on leaders because there are very few leadership roles that do not require increasing levels of resilience with the accelerating pace of change.

To build a resilient organization, we need three things:

1. A leader who understands how to build a resilience framework (and preferably has done this work themselves).

2. Alignment around where the team or organization is going and what it will take to get there.

3. A resilience framework for the organization around which everyone is aligned.

The types of challenges leaders and organizations face in today's world are more complex, and they involve more diverse stakeholders.

These kinds of challenges require our teams and organizations to create solutions that require us to think differently–*radically* differently–while seeking to understand and mobilize an increasing array of stakeholders in ways we may never have had to mobilize before. These *adaptive* challenges require more than "business as usual" solutions. Often, defining the challenge itself *is* the challenge and frequently even *that* requires tradeoffs in values and loyalties that require us to manage what the organization is losing.

In Part One we talked about the importance of distinguishing between two types of challenges facing leaders and organizations: **Technical** challenges that are resolved by applying expertise; and **adaptive** challenges that require thinking differently. The distinction is an important one because a different type of leadership will be called for–a different way of thinking–depending upon the kind of challenge being faced: Is it technical or adaptive in nature?

It is very important that the people around us *also* understand that solving adaptive challenges requires thinking differently. Frequently, the more complex and ambiguous nature of adaptive challenges requires resilience. The components of the Resilience Framework, then, must be created for the team. This is why alignment is so important.

Adaptive challenges frequently require shifts in leaders' expectations of the leaders who report to them and the teams that report to those leaders. Getting aligned around those challenges and new expectations, why they are critical, and what must be different, is a crucial first step.

A top 5 global bank could not seem to decide if the Merchant Services business was a business they wanted to sell or keep. At least once a year, they would put in the next hot new Ivy League MBA they had hired to run it just to see what they could do. This resulted in a lot of churn as the new business President always brought in a new leadership team, except for the Learning (training) function. No one seemed to care about bringing in a favorite head of Learning. And so, I stayed longer than most.

After about a year working with the Merchant Business, I became the most tenured person on the team. This was laughable because while I knew a LOT about developing executives, I knew precious little about the day to day business. My team, however, did.

One day, while trying to launch a new product, the leadership team realized that everyone in the business who had ever done pricing was gone. There was not a single person on the team who could price the product and figure out profitable deals for the Sales department to sell. They were lost.

It seemed insane to assign this to Learning, but committed to figuring it out, I called my team together. Because of all the disruption in the business, we had met a couple of months prior, brainstormed ideas, and prepared ourselves for the day when we might need to jump in on a moment's notice—we just didn't know where or when. My team understood even more than I did that each time a leader left, valuable institutional knowledge was lost. Because they were attuned to this problem, they had begun to document the knowledge before it was lost, without my direction.

They were beyond excited to be asked to contribute. It didn't matter that this would be a second full-time job; they were energized by the challenge. It turned out that two of them had learned more about pricing than anyone else in the business. Until we could get the new leaders up to speed, the Learning Team became Learning and Pricing. And the new product got launched.

That team jumped at the chance to be heroes. They were energized and the business was elevated. Learning earned new respect that year because that team of rock stars ran some scenarios and got aligned long before they needed to. They believed they could help even though they had been marginalized in the past. They mobilized, filled up their tanks and worked double time until the clear purpose of equipping the business to price deals without help was achieved. And they did this without a lot of input from their leader. That's what resilient teams do.

Building an Organizational Resilience Framework

If we have taken the time to learn the Leader*Shift®* Resilience Framework and build individual resilience, we can leverage those same skills to build a resilient team.

The characteristics of both resilient individuals and organizations are the same and we can begin to build them the *exact* same way in our sphere of influence. There is, however, one crucial additional step that will ensure that the resilience you build in an organization actually "sticks" and is sustainable over time.

Aligned Teams and Organizations Stay Resilient

These teams are aligned to a cause, a purpose or a broader strategy. Creating alignment is a leader's first critical focus. Part Two explains how to apply the framework we used to build *individual* resilience in Part One to the teams we lead.

If the stress that drove you to pick up a book on Resilience is caused by your organization, know that while we may not be able to change the whole thing, we can definitely influence the pieces that we touch or lead.

To review the model through the lens of leading a team:

An organization's ability to be resilient is a result of its mindset and its choices. Mindset is still a function of authenticity and attitude and choices are still a function of the organization's purpose and how it defines success. Underlying all of that is a set of core beliefs.

Resilience IS A RESULT OF:

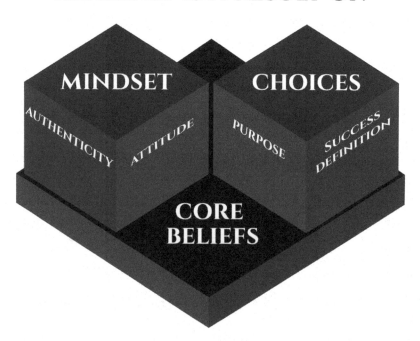

LeaderShift® Resilience Framework

This summary can be translated slightly to: An organization's ability to be resilient is a result of it's culture and the decisions it makes. Culture is a function of authenticity and what it feels like to work there. Decisions are a function of the purpose, mission and values.

No matter what you call it, the components of resilience are the same for individuals and organizations. Organizations simply require a few more people to become aligned, and this is not something a leader can do behind a closed door.

The Corporate Climate

It is no longer enough to do things better, faster and cheaper.

Many of us are exhausted by the systemic drama of the organizations for which we work. Corporate life is tough. Leaders get knocked down, spread thin and asked to deliver more than ever before. It's hard to be adaptive when we are exhausted.

A reminder from Part One: Corporate leaders are the most over-worked athletes in the world.

In most cases, leaders are *also* responsible for results not owned by anyone else, and, in addition to leading, they also have a "real job": They are accountable for their *own* results. And in the heat of the struggle for results, which of a leader's more-than-full-time jobs suffers? Here's a clue: it's not results.

What suffers most is the *quality of leadership* when things get tough, busy or otherwise disrupted. It's a vicious circle, because the minute the disruption hits, the quality of "life" for members of that leader's team diminishes–quickly. When people are under stress (even stress that perceived as positive), results suffer, creating more of a struggle, just at the moment when better leadership is needed. This will happen unless they are resilient and can be energized and elevated by the struggle.

Sound familiar?

"To lead is to live dangerously."

– Ron Heifetz and Marty Linsky

In the jacket of their book, *Leadership on The Line*, Ron Heifetz and Marty Linsky tell us that, "Real leadership–the kind that surfaces conflict, challenges long-held beliefs, and demands new ways of doing things–causes pain. And when people feel threatened, they take aim at the person pushing for change. As a result, leaders often get hurt both personally and professionally." That is why building resilience is so critical in the face of adaptive work. In politics, we call this assassination, but there are a million other ways to get assassinated or derailed in corporations without getting shot.

Warning: Adaptive leadership requires
leaders to ask the tough questions.

Often, those questions are the ones people are thinking silently to themselves or the politically unsafe questions they dare not ask out loud. They are the questions that surface undercurrents of contradictions in values and behaviors, or in strategy and decisions. Sometimes these questions can pick at the scabs of hypocrisy. They may be critical to the end goal but to those in charge are "better left unsaid". These kinds of questions can cause some people to face potential losses and might print a big red target on our own heads. The need for resilience is underscored by these corporate realities: It is only a matter of time before an adaptive leader will have to make personal choices about their purpose and demonstrate how important it is to remain in the fight.

Traditional "big boss" leadership defaults to having someone in charge make decisions and then tell people what to do, but in the face of more complex adaptive challenges, this approach can fail miserably. Adaptive challenges require leaders to exercise a more inclusive style of leadership–mobilizing people to collaborate to solve problems or face opportunities when there is not a clear path forward–*because* these challenges are too big to be solved by one person's expertise (even if they have been a "big boss").

With the increasing pace of change today in organizations, leaders and teams are facing adaptive challenges more and more.

Some of the adaptive challenges we are seeing include:

- An organization must transform from the inside out to leverage new technology and the data it provides. A commercial real estate firm had to rethink the way they build relationships as customers' buying decisions became more data driven and less relationship-based. As competitors increased the amount of information they provided customers, the deep, long-term relationships that seasoned sales reps had built took a back seat to the market data the customers now demanded. Imagine the kinds of tradeoffs required by the sales person whose history is no longer as effective as how well he analyzes data or uses technology. This changes the ideal candidate HR must now recruit into the sales department. Imagine the shifts in incentives, organization structure, and training that will also be required, and the demotivation of people who have been valued for something that may no longer be relevant.

- A team must put their heads together to figure out how to deal with a market disruptor. Imagine the leadership team of a small retail store needing to find new revenue streams as Amazon enters the market, or a large multinational bank having to compete with new, more nimble, accessible and lower-cost payment options like Square or PayPal. Expertise in brick and mortar stores that once brought them success will no longer sustain a future where customers are online and can shop from anywhere.

- A company that has grown by acquisition reaches the tipping point where they can't increase the value beyond the sum of the acquired companies without consolidating, finding synergy and creating an aligned organization. This team, often in banking or financial services, must figure out how to build a future bigger than any one leader's previous vision. This likely will require everyone to deal with losses and shifts as they integrate products, services and learn to make decisions differently. Skillsets will need to change, and again for some, the things that got them where they are will not get them the results they need in the new organization.

- A leader is promoted and now must now lead the team of which she was once a part. This requires changes in relationships—potentially losses—and shifts in behavior and thinking for everyone on the team. The leader's success will depend on her ability to drive big changes in how people relate to one another effectively.

- A team is suddenly asked to deliver more with less. Where the team was able to "get by" before, the margin of error and free time are now shrinking. Often, when resources get tight, it exposes an employee who is not taking full ownership of their role. A leader in this situation stands to lose personal credibility, suffer losses in team performance–as well sanity– if they cannot motivate and lead everyone on their team to take personal responsibility for their results.

Wrapping It Up

Applying the Leader*Shift*® Resilience Framework to a team or organization is as simple as bringing the team together to carefully consider and plan for each component of the framework as it relates to the team. We use it in two ways: First, as a check-list to ensure that all the pieces are in place to be resilient before we need them; Second, as a reminder or guide when disruption hits and urgent decisions need to be made. When complete, the framework acts as a compass pointing towards the organization's strategic "true north."

Building an organizational Resilience Framework takes effort, collaboration and discipline. It sometimes takes picking at some old scabs, getting blood flowing, and building excitement to flex muscles and exert strength. It takes time, but if facilitated properly, the process requires less time than you might expect.

We have streamlined this process effectively for many companies and it can be integrated into (not separate from) the daily work that needs to happen to drive business. There are few bonding exercises more meaningful for a team than going through this process. And there is no confidence builder more powerful for a team that needs to take on the world, than knowing they *can*.

Apply it right now

Using the Leader*Shift*® Resilience Framework as a checklist:

- Put a check mark over the components that you believe the people on your team would say the team or organization has got right.

- Circle the components that you believe would be unclear or evaluated differently by different groups of people.

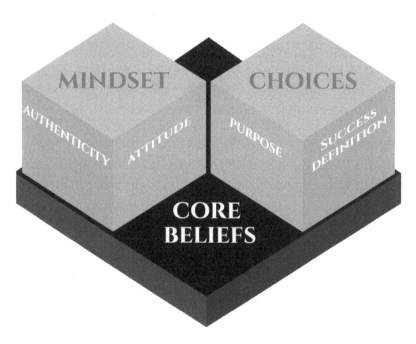

Resilience IS A RESULT OF:

- Ask a few colleagues or a confidante to comment on your thoughts and push back on your thinking.

- Underline the components that need the most work.

- Share this framework with your team and ask where they think there are gaps in the team's resilience.

Take It with You

- Adaptive challenges and rapid disruptive change have made building resilient teams and organizations increasingly more critical.

- The Leader*Shift*® Resilience Framework can be applied to building resilient teams.

- An organization's ability to be resilient is a result of its culture and the decisions it makes. Culture is a function of authenticity and what it feels like to work there. Decisions are a function of the organization's purpose, mission and core values.

- Team alignment is crucial for incorporating *sustained* resilience.

CHAPTER 12

The First Step: Create Alignment

"Alignment is the essence of management."

– Fred Smith, Chairman of FedEx

Hearing a message that we have a responsibility to create resilient organizations can be tough, especially if the need for resilience is caused by our organization in the first place. Misaligned organizations can be brutal. Working in a misaligned organization causes the kind of stress that requires people to try and *cope*, which is not the same thing as being resilient.

Resilient Organizations Are Aligned

Most great leaders are not afraid of challenges–they want to work in a place where they can tackle tough challenges–but almost none of them want to take on stupid ones. Nobody wants to waste time figuring out how to do business or compete *within* the organization simply because people are not on the same page. Misalignment causes stress, distraction, and pain. Not all of us have the scope to be able to fix our entire organization, but we can get our teams aligned.

Alignment is the first step to building a resilient team or organization, because creating a Resilience Framework with a broader group of people requires alignment. By the time we get there, we want to be able to focus on building resilience, not on having to get on the same page.

If our team is called upon to tackle adaptive challenges, we are going to need to be resilient.

Last year, I got a call from a consumer products company looking for someone to facilitate a "hash-it-out" session with the leadership team. The company wanted help creating "new norms" for how they would work together. The team wasn't getting along. The CEO had assumed the role, replacing someone who had a much more domineering leadership style. She couldn't understand why her team members looked to her to solve all their issues and make all the strategic decisions. And, of course, there was a bully. There usually is. This one was in Finance.

Business Operations and Sales were in direct competition for resources. Leaders of support functions didn't have a chance of being heard. And amid all the stress, turnover in the critical General Manager (GM) role was increasing and they just couldn't seem to find the right talent.

All this was happening while massive changes were taking place in the market. This team was allowing the "ship" to be tossed around in a rough sea rather than hoisting its sails together and catching the wind. The CEO was hanging on by a proverbial thread and now wanted to hash it out and create new norms.

We did what no self-respecting consulting firm trying to make money would. We refused.

Because we knew what they wanted to do wouldn't work and we were aligned: We were more interested in positive outcomes than we were in making money.

There are almost no situations where "hashing it out," by itself, solves anything. There was a reason why this team had gotten into this mess and that reason alone would threaten its ability to be resilient in the long term. Without addressing that root cause, "hashing it out" sessions are a waste of time; new team norms will never be more than a page in a binder.

One of this team's biggest problems was the opportunity cost of the energy being spent: internal competition; hidden agendas; dealing with the bully; scraping and clawing for credibility; and just generally plotting against each other. Until that team is willing to stop the work-avoiding activities of hashing, blaming, and "scapegoating" and come to terms with what is driving it, they will continue to struggle.

Lack of Alignment Shifts the Focus Off Driving Strategy

Imagine what might happen if all that energy were being spent on working together towards a common goal. Imagine how much better equipped that team would be. To be able to stand up on the surfboard and ride the waves of change and business challenges coming at them, instead of being slammed into the sand and crushed by them. Imagine how little they would need to focus on team norms if people were all on the same page.

That's resilience.

And it cannot happen when leaders and teams are not aligned.

"The task of leadership is to create an alignment of strengths, making a system's weaknesses irrelevant."

– Peter Drucker

Would you want to work at a company where everyone from the CEO to the unpaid intern comes to work knowing EXACTLY what they need to do, even on those days where plans fail, and crises happen? A place where everyone pitches in and departments cover for one another, even when someone messes up? A place where there is no blame or infighting, but instead, healthy and constant creative collaboration? A place where decisions are made through the same lens, with an intentional choice of filters that people understand, articulate and support? One where the underlying company mood is a sense of grand adventure and excitement and where collaboration is the norm?

That's what can be expected. And it has a name - it is called **Alignment**.

Aligned organizations can be truly amazing places to work. They have five characteristics in common and they build them in this order:

1. They Create a Shared Agenda

2. They Leverage The Culture (Filters) to Drive Strategy

3. They Have an Aligned Structure

4. They Have a Shared Investment Roadmap

5. They Have Best Talent Driving the Most Critical Capabilities

If you are curious about how aligned your organization is, take the Leader*Shift*® Alignment Quiz with our compliments at www. Leader*Shift*Insights.com.

1. They Create a Shared Agenda

The first step leadership teams in aligned organizations take is to create alignment around a shared agenda for the team and with the rest of the organization. This can be done on a smaller scale with a team as well. All leaders can do this with their teams.

Notice the word, "create." We don't "get" alignment. We *create* alignment. There is an enormous difference. A shared agenda is created *together.* It isn't "sold" or forced on people. We don't need to "get buy-in." It's a colossal waste of time which is avoided entirely when people share building the agenda in the first place. Those conversations can be a wrestling match, but with clear intention, they are approached head-on instead of avoided. They are not "hash-out" sessions. Instead, they are rich with debate during which everyone down to the most junior person is heard. Ideas can come from anywhere and that junior person needs to understand how decisions are made. This process allows for contrasting opinions without promulgating conflict.

However, we often hear objections. Frequently, there is a very real fear that bringing people to the table will open a "Pandora's box" of interpersonal drama: One person has a personal agenda; another will dominate the conversation; one will shut down and another will be upset. Leaders are often afraid that once the proverbial box is open, they won't be able to get the lid back on and resolve anything. This is NOT a reason not to open the box. Leaving the lid closed and not discussing the real issues merely creates pressure that will eventually blow the box (and the team) apart.

Instead, create alignment around the most overarching or high-level issues first, moving down toward the most contentious. We use this approach when designing organization structures and have found it to be akin to a superpower. If diverse and sometimes disparate stakeholders can agree on things like a two to three year future state, over-arching criteria, guiding principles, value proposition, who the customers are, and what the organization must be able to do to serve them, by the time they get to more sensitive topics like structure, they are nearly diffused because the answer, by then, has become obvious to all.

If you aren't comfortable doing this with your team, get help. Don't avoid it if you need to build resilience. A skilled, objective facilitator is worth the investment.

Shared agendas blow hidden agendas out of the water.

The act of creating a shared agenda, by definition, eliminates personal or hidden agendas. It is the fastest way to pull everyone onto the same page. It creates a mechanism and holds the group accountable to it. Sometimes, a shared agenda needs only be a list of problems the team is united in solving. Sometimes it is alignment around a future state or *mission*, so that everyone has some skin in the game around the organization's direction. And sometimes, it is alignment around the capabilities the organization must deliver to drive its strategy and a clear set of priorities.

When a shared agenda is created, it can be waved like a flag leading troops into battle, a unifying rallying cry. In an aligned organization, even those who may disagree with the agenda understand *why* the agenda is what it has become. Everyone can articulate it in their own words, making it come alive rather than remain stoically framed on a wall.

This process takes about two days. We think resilience is worth that.

$$\ast \;\; \ast \;\; \ast \;\; \ast \;\; \ast$$

Not long ago, we facilitated a meeting with the IT Security department for a large retail company to create alignment around a desired future state.

The company had experienced a major security breach and a new leader was brought in to close a capability gap around IT Security. As the meeting progressed, the group divided into smaller teams to brainstorm ideas for the future of the IT Security Function.

The first two teams reported out lots of details, envisioning how to grow their credibility and the function. It was clear that growing the organization was very important to one or two of the participants. These were "up and comers" who wanted to grow their teams, have lots of direct reports, and were passionate about protecting the company from another data breach.

The third group to report out chose a young woman who was clearly new to the company as its spokesperson. She quietly began, "We have a different idea." She went on to explain her belief that if they were truly successful at building world class IT security, they would not need to or want to grow the team. Instead, success would look like a smaller function with systems and technology so effective, it would not require so many people. She finished speaking, and in an instant, the group shifted. There was simply no way to promote a personal agenda of growing a team when no one could deny that a smaller function would indicate success.

As a result, a shared agenda was born: Create world class technology that would put the IT Security Function out of business.

$$\ast \ \ast \ \ast \ \ast \ \ast$$

Once the shared agenda is created there is no opting out. There is no dissent if an agenda is truly shared. Together the organization moves forward. Decision making is aligned. It is fast, focused, and people are accountable to each other.

2. They Leverage The Culture (Filters) to Drive Strategy

Just as each of us has a set of filters through which we view the world, organizations have filters too. We call the sum of organizational filters its culture. These are the unspoken criteria by which decisions are made or how work gets done. These filters may be subtle, but nowhere is an organization's culture more apparent than at town hall meetings when senior leaders speak to the employees. Much can be learned about how both the leaders and employees handle those interactions.

Aligned organizations understand the kind of culture and organizational filters they need in order to deliver the capabilities required to drive the strategy. They've done the work to understand the gap between the future vision and the current reality and are making intentional strides to build a culture that removes distractions from delivering results. For the aligned organization, discussing its filters (both the intentional and unintentional ones), is a part of doing business.

Much has been written about Larry Bossidy, best-selling author and former CEO of AlliedSignal, and his "larger than life" leadership style. When he was CEO of AlliedSignal, employees would not consider missing his "town hall meetings." These sessions were informal and frequent. He took open questions from the floor and it didn't matter if it was a 20-year veteran administrative assistant complaining about her vacation benefits or a question from a new Vice President about a strategy in Singapore; he answered them. If Larry didn't have the answer, he found someone who did, often right there on the spot. There was no question Larry was afraid to hear or answer publicly. If you were called on from the audience and you had an intelligent question or a good response to something he asked on the fly, it was a real feather in your cap.

At a different but well-known global manufacturing company, before a town hall meeting, teams were told very strictly that instead of asking questions, they were to find the answer privately, so as not to put executives on the spot. Town hall meetings there were a carefully scripted show, with everything from the location to who sat where, all very carefully orchestrated, staged and broadcast to employees around the world. There was as much messaging in the positioning of seats as there was in what was presented.

At a large technology company, town hall meetings were a forum for the CEO to berate, call out, or humiliate executives in areas that weren't performing well. The only thing worse than having to attend and watch this was not attending and getting slammed publicly for not being there.

The filters of the CEO or leader cascade throughout the organization or team whether those leaders want them to or not. At AlliedSignal, you could speak your mind and be respected for it because Larry Bossidy operated with a filter of *openness.* The result was that issues were dealt with quickly and rarely distracted from results when the organization needed resilience.

At the manufacturing company above, however, issues were dealt with behind the scenes and the politics were often difficult to decipher. This was most likely because its leaders dealt with *nothing* in public; the meeting before the meeting was more important than the meeting. A lot of effort was wasted on managing image, perceptions and sorting through politics. Organizational politics is an enormous distraction at many organizations. Imagine if all that energy were spent on beating the competition instead of beating each other *inside* the organization.

Internal politics destroys resilience.

At the technology company, public humiliation was rampant at every level, starting from the top and oozing all the way down. Think about that from the lens of driving innovation: Fear always votes, "no." This organization brought in a new CEO who had to eliminate and replace a lot of the leadership team to stop the humiliation and create an environment more conducive to innovation. Imagine the cost, effort and disruption of firing, sourcing and hiring several C-level leaders. Imagine the institutional knowledge that walked out the door and the long-term effects on the culture of humiliating people. That had to shift to make people feel safe enough to innovate again. All of that subtracts from an organization's ability to be resilient. Leadership churn and the way we treat people matters.

For these reasons, one of the best assessments of organizational culture is a personal values assessment of its leaders. Unless they intentionally focus on building a specific culture and understand the behaviors required to do that, by default, leaders create cultures that reflect their own personal values—and they may not even be aware of it.

It's that pesky human nature thing again.

You cannot teach what you do not know.
You cannot lead where you will not go.

There are companies making millions assessing organizational culture. When clients come to us with cultural issues, we save them a lot of money by recommending the following: Understand the capabilities required to drive your strategy and the kind of culture that will be required to deliver them efficiently. Then, to understand the organization's culture, get to know the motives, values and culture preferences of the company's top 10 leaders. The patterns that emerge when you compare the leadership team's values will tell you all you need to know and precisely how to change it.

Organizational culture is *measured* from the bottom up, but it is always *driven* from the top down. All the culture teams, assessments and millions of dollars spent on consulting projects will not change that.

3. They Have an Aligned Structure

The third thing aligned organizations have in common is a structure that supports its ability to *deliver* the shared agenda. In many (if not, most) organizations, organizational structures have been built out of necessity. They landed there because they just *did*, rather than because of any intentional *planning*.

Sometimes work is assigned to a leader who has the capacity or skills to take on the task, rather than putting the work in the appropriate place, the place that makes the most sense to deliver a capability efficiently or most effectively. Often, work is assigned as a "special project" or given to an employee the organization is seeking to develop. Sometimes, a leader gets away with hoarding people and work to build a personal "empire," because no one else will fight them for it. And, sometimes, work comes in as part of an acquisition and gets "bolted on" to the quickest, easiest place. None of these things are inherently bad, they are just not intentional. And they lead to misaligned companies.

These "happenstance" structures are fine unless they keep your organization from being resilient. These structures increase the opportunity cost by making things difficult, while decreasing margin, or inhibiting you from achieving the strategy. Any of these approaches (or happenstances) may work for a while, but as an organization grows, this catches up and results in silos. Silos have a way of becoming kingdoms within the organization, complete with walls to keep others out.

"Every organization is perfectly tuned
to deliver exactly the results it gets."

– Arthur Jones

Imagine an organization where decisions are made at the exact point in the process where they need to be made, instead of elevated for approval. Delegating decisions upwards is not only a waste of time, it's a strategy sinker. Imagine that everyone has a clear understanding of the capabilities the organization must deliver to create a differentiated customer experience. Imagine real alignment around where the gaps are and what must be done to fix them. Imagine having a set of priorities that you know will drive the strategy, that aren't up for debate, and with which the right things are done even without asking and even across functions. It is possible. That is what an aligned structure delivers. It can even be designed to be adaptive.

Many years ago, while building the RapidOD approach to organizational design, we worked with a sales leadership team for a large consumer products company. RapidOD, at the time, was revolutionary. It still is. It is a fast, collaborative and inclusive approach to organizational design that starts with strategy, the customer, and business model, to ensure that the structure will, in fact, drive strategy. This process has formed the basis for much of our consulting business.

We discovered that the company had recently created a new phone list for its retail store clients. The list contained 38 phone numbers and made it easier to understand who to call for whatever product or service was needed. The team was incredibly proud of its efforts to get the list down from over 50 customer contact people.

*How many contact people do you think the customer wanted? Let me assure you, it was not a list of 38. Upon a bit of investigation, we found that the customers wanted **one** number – they didn't want a list.*

This approach allowed the team to effectively create a single point of contact for the customer, a shared agenda around what the customer experience should look and feel like, and aligned the structure to drive it. The approach has evolved since then, but the win created on that project launched RapidOD to a recognizable and frequently requested approach to designing organizations that "get it right the first time."

When an organization structure is aligned to deliver the capabilities required to drive an organization's strategy, there is less distraction. The priorities are clear, and less time is spent wondering who does what, or figuring out how to get things approved (or worse, waiting on approvals), or arguing across functions and steering focus away from delivering results. When it is time demonstrate resilience, organizations with aligned structures collaborate better, move more efficiently and act more innovatively than those that waste energy figuring out how to "do business with themselves."

Structures that evolve over time can work. People eventually hang around long enough to figure out how work gets done. But when market disruption hits, margins get tight and it is time to be resilient, structure matters. Period.

4. They Have a Shared Investment Roadmap

The fourth component aligned organizations share is alignment around *investment priorities* and the assurance that the next investment made will directly contribute most significantly to the business strategy. While there could be (and should be) much debate (discussion in creating and validating it on some regular cadence), a prioritized investment roadmap removes the distracting static or infighting caused by constant internal competition for resources. It also encourages collaborative work across organizational boundaries or silos.

A fast-growing technology company had acquired several small companies and asked for help figuring out how to integrate and align around a future state for the company and how to get there. The leadership team was comprised of a blend of people from each company. They were young, aggressive, sharp and quite appropriately, had very little tolerance for wasting time and a mountain of work today.

I got 30 minutes with the CFO ahead of time and the first thing she said to me was that they "were aligned." Everyone knew what needed to happen and she didn't like or need consultants–people just needed to do their jobs. She explained how they had hired the best people, and everyone knew what they were doing.

I asked a few questions and quickly learned that the functions in the organization were siloed. They were so busy, they didn't have time to work together. Sales was busy selling and product was building products. IT was trying to integrate the infrastructure.

The problem was that IT wasn't working on the infrastructure for the product that the product team was working on and that sales was selling a product they might not be able to deliver, and that marketing was working on something else, entirely.

We worked with the team to create alignment around the capabilities that would be required to deliver the business strategy and then to build a prioritized investment roadmap. This ensured that each project and investment was sequenced and slotted over time with dependencies in the right place. It also ensured that areas that were prioritized first were the ones with most critical contribution to the strategy. Suddenly, the team got on the same page. It wasn't that they didn't know what they were doing, they simply weren't aligned around priorities and it was creating confusion. This distracted from the ability to be resilient when the team's biggest disruptor was the need to integrate and build a new organization that could compete effectively.

Aligning around an investment roadmap eliminates internal competition for resources, ensuring that the focus is on the right priorities and that they are clear to everyone.

Infighting and competition have been the death of many a team and have threatened many personal and corporate relationships. There is no need for that when the energy is better focused on setting the organization up to be more competitive against the real, external competition. When we get the priorities "right," the organization does not have to waste time debating every investment by itself. And they have criteria to determine when they should invest, and in what.

Think of an organization with clear investment priorities where each project, investment, or resource expenditure—including people—is evaluated based on its contribution to delivering the organization's strategy or shared agenda. What if we were able to see, over the next three years, a clear plan that ensured that the next investment was the most critical? And to complete the picture, what if everyone in the organization were *aligned* to that plan?

Instead of setting shared priorities and direction, there are leaders who believe that forcing internal competition and pitting one executive against another is productive. I've even seen one tactic where two leaders are secretly assigned the same project by a CEO who wanted to see who would do it better or faster. That may sound like an interesting exercise, but just imagine the benefits of those two highly qualified leaders working together. Imagine their frustration when they find out they've been "had"? What does that do to engagement?

Creating dysfunctional competition may have worked when companies had extra people on the payroll to keep busy, but it does not work in an uncertain or ambiguous environment. In a world where margins are shrinking and staying ahead takes everything we can throw at it, this old school approach is a waste of time and energy and is *destructive* to an organization. To be blunt: It's a stupid approach designed to cover up a leader's inability to drive collaboration and be adaptive and it has an extremely high long-term cost to the dynamics of the organization and the people within it.

In our experience, organizations benefit most when people are aligned around a clear roadmap of priorities and investments that accelerate delivering the strategy.

5. They Have Best Talent Driving the Most Critical Capabilities

The last thing that aligned organizations have in common is that they are very particular about who runs what. This doesn't mean that the CEO's favorite employee runs the branch overlooking the beach in Oahu. It means that the *highest performers own the most critical things* the organization needs to get right to deliver the strategy. We call those critical things strategic *organizational capabilities.*

Organizational capabilities are identified based on what must be done to deliver the strategy. But they are not all created equal. For example, we can optimize the heck out of Payroll and it won't drive a dime of revenue. You want your best people running the capabilities that drive a differentiated customer experience and have the potential to contribute financially or drive strategy.

* * * * *

After helping an insurance company create alignment around the capabilities they would need to drive its strategy, we asked them to prioritize those capabilities. We took them through a simple and fast process to identify what would be needed to create differentiation in the future, which capabilities had the highest financial contribution, as well as the gaps they had at the time. As the impact of the Affordable Care Act was still unclear, we asked them to consider several possible scenarios. Leadership determined that it was highly likely they would need to enter a market they had thus far avoided. Medicaid works differently from the other products this company knew well, so it would be new territory for them, and it was critical.

At the same time, the organization assessed its structure and talent. We led a process to calibrate performance ratings that resulted in a talent planning session. For the first time, the leadership team that was used to operating in silos, shared information about the talent on each of their teams. Some of them knew the top talent, but until they had a frank conversation, they hadn't aligned around those most critical to develop and retain—their business-critical talent.

As a result of that discussion, the team realized that there was a high performing executive whose role was to be eliminated due to the structure changes. He was someone they wanted to retain AND was someone they all trusted. Because he reported to another executive, the head of Product Development didn't realize he had worked on Medicaid in his role at a former company. Shifting him into another area gave the leadership team a chance to send a message that he was valued and to provide him an exciting new challenge. AND it saved the time, money and distraction of having to let a senior employee go and find someone else with a different skillset.

If you're trying to build a resilient organization, talent management conversations *always* make sense. The more we get to know the people outside our immediate area, figure out how well they're doing, and understand their expertise, the faster we can figure out where to turn when we need those skills in the midst of a disruptive change. Creating alignment around business-critical talent is the first step in talent management but ensuring that those people are put charge of your most critical capabilities is what really leads to resilience. It fills the tank.

It's important to note that when we assign ownership of a critical capability to our best talent, we must also grant them the authority to make the decisions required to deliver it. Business transformation expert Keith Leust, author of *The Business Transformation Field Book*, calls this a "single throat to choke." He believes that it's critical that someone the organization trusts has both the visibility and responsibility for the most critical capabilities. It's also important to know *who* those people are and who you want them to become in the future. There are many books written on this topic and the authors of this one have spent many years implementing talent and succession programs.

The right talent in the right place at the right time is critical to delivering your business strategy.

Wrapping It Up

Socrates said, "The unexamined life is not worth living."

Likewise, the authors believe the unaligned business is not worth building. Because disruption happens. And it's called disruption because it's usually unexpected, unplanned, and you're unprepared for it.

Building resilience requires creating alignment across the spectrum of leaders, teams and people as well, since only aligned organizations will ever become resilient in the long-term.

Creating alignment (*real* alignment) requires intention. It demands a collaborative effort to drive clarity around a shared agenda, culture, structure, investments and talent that drives strategy. An aligned organization is better equipped to begin to become resilient because building each component of the Resilience Framework requires alignment, too.

Apply It Right Now

Given the five areas of alignment, check the ones that you feel your team is aligned around. Remember that by "aligned" we mean that they could clearly articulate the current state, how it is linked to the strategy AND understand why each piece is critical. In addition, each member of the team is clear on how their role drives toward the strategy and how they can support one another.

☐ A shared strategic agenda is in place

☐ People understand the culture (filters) and leverage it intentionally to drive strategy

☐ The structure is aligned to drive strategy

☐ A shared investment roadmap exists and is clear

☐ The best talent is driving the most critical capabilities the organization needs to deliver

Taking It with You

- Creating alignment is a critical first step to building a resilient organization

- There are five key areas where alignment is critical. Aligned organizations:

  1. Have created a shared strategic agenda that every leader can clearly articulate. This agenda explains where they are going, the capabilities they need to deliver, and how they will do that.

  2. Understand the culture and organizational filters today. They know what filters need to be in place to deliver the strategy. They understand the gaps and are working to intentionally shape and leverage this culture to drive strategy.

  3. They have an aligned structure so that work gets done as efficiently and effectively as possible.

  4. They have a shared Investment Roadmap so priorities and dependencies are clear. They are confident that the next investment will make the greatest contribution to driving the strategy.

  5. They have the best talent in the organization driving the most critical capabilities.

- Without front-end alignment, back-end resilience is out of reach

CHAPTER 13

Create A Resilient Team Mindset

Resilience IS A RESULT OF:

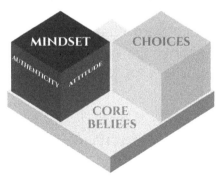

"Authentic leadership is revealed in the alignment of what you think, what you say, and what you do."

– Michael Holland

In the same way we focus on shaping our individual mindsets to build resilience, we can mold a healthy mindset within our team or organization.

Mindset is a function of authenticity and attitude in organizations as well. Authentic organizations are trustworthy, and their employees tend to be loyal; people are loyal to those they trust. This is critical to resilience because resilience is all about being able to pull on that extra discretionary effort (reserve in the tank) when we need it. Loyal people give more discretionary effort because they are not distracted by worrying about whether they can trust the organization during disruption.

An organization's attitude has a lot to do with its culture, brand, and what it's like to work there. Organizations with a resilient attitude drive focus to delivering what's important. They minimize the distractions that cause needless churn so that no energy is spent on what isn't important.

Organizational Authenticity & Attitude

Authenticity and attitude are essential components of creating a mindset that drives resilience.

We can think of an organization's culture as its mindset and it has a lot to do with how well people work together and make decisions. It has to do with how organized or chaotic an organization is, what it's like to work there, and whether the focus is on the team or the individual. We don't often talk about organizational culture quite this way, but the same components of an individual's mindset can be viewed through a corporate lens.

There is a simple and sometimes humorous test we have used with clients who want to test whether people really believe or live the things the organization says about itself, its "party line." We use the "snicker test" to measure authenticity. Before we prepare to bring a group of leaders together to create alignment around an organization or team's future state, we ask for the documents and "cultural artifacts" they already have developed. Things like the mission, vision, values, principles...all the things that show up in fancy graphics lining the walls of conference rooms and offices. At one company it was a cheer people recited. At another, it was a set of principles that appeared in every presentation.

The snicker test is simple. We collect all the artifacts, put them on a table and ask people to think of the last five decisions that were made by their team, boss or leadership. Then we ask, in light of those decisions, which of what you see, makes you snicker. The exercise requires a courageous leader and bit of preparation to create a safe space for people to speak, but in the end, we've yet to meet a CEO that wouldn't like to know where the organization is not being authentic. And if asked, employees will tell us.

To figure out where the organization is going, we must figure out where it is right now, today. It's difficult to undertake any endeavor—whether it's a trip or a change initiative—if we don't know our starting point.

The snicker test can prompt, well, snickers. But it has a very serious purpose. When something fails the snicker test, it indicates an organization is actively projecting to the world an image that is different from the reality of living in its culture. This is a problem, not only because it is a reason for employees to snicker, but also because the effort spent keeping up an image that isn't real will eventually do two things: It will threaten the brand and it will distract from the strategy.

It is inevitable that eventually there will be a need for either the employees or customers to trust the organization's value proposition, its brand promise. If leadership is known to project one image while the organization lives another, that brand promise, whether to customers who have seen the artifacts or employees who snicker, is broken. When that leadership needs the trust of their people or their customers to deal with an emerging crisis and that trust isn't there, they are sunk.

Second, both the effort spent snickering coupled with the time spent talking about *why*, remove the focus from delivering the organization's strategy and place it somewhere else. There is nothing productive that can come of that. At some point, an organization will face disruption like an adaptive challenge and will need all the discretionary energy it has built up in the reserve tank. When people are distracted by an image that isn't real, that tank registers empty fast. Employees trust leaders and organization who do what they say they will do. When they don't, loyalty suffers. Snickers are a good indication of that.

As we know from our personal work, authenticity and time spent "hiding" behind an image happens in organizations, too. The market can fuel corporate authenticity when an organization's behaviors and visible decisions are in alignment with who or what the organization says it is. Remember how Johnson & Johnson handled the tainted

Tylenol scandal? Seven people died from malevolent tampering. But the organization's senior leadership, headed by chairman James Burke, formed a strategy team and began *not* with the question "how do we save the product and our profits?" but rather with the question, "how do we protect the people?" The result is a case study in successful, proactive, authentic leadership.

Because these behaviors and decisions are made by people, in larger companies, organizational authenticity can only happen when leaders are on the same page.

When AlliedSignal, a fully integrated conglomerate with a Metro New York, hierarchical, "take-the-hill" leadership style, acquired Honeywell, a midwestern, consensus driven, portfolio company, the new company could not move forward until it reconciled how to integrate these two vastly different cultures. The company had to figure out "who it was going to be" when it "grew up." Sadly, the merger consultants they hired decided to skip this part and things went horribly awry.

Honeywell spent several years spinning its wheels, losing money, and bleeding talent. Hundreds of highly talented people jumped ship from AlliedSignal's former headquarters in Morristown, NJ. Eventually, the board fired a CEO and brought leaders back from retirement to put the pieces back together. The organization had to work backwards – wasting time recreating processes and muddling through massive cultural differences – before it could move forward as the new Honeywell.

All this because they didn't focus on culture and getting the mindset right in the first place.

I was in that room in Morristown when the big-name, highly-paid consultant in the fancy suit told us we were going to "simply ignore culture and focus on integrating processes." I'll never forget that. I was perhaps 25 years old at the time and I wanted to throw up. We all knew better.

A merger of two enormous (and highly successful) corporations, came very close to failing and the company would have been bought by a third company had the SEC not stepped in. It disrupted tens of thousands of jobs and countless lives because they didn't create alignment around the new organization's culture. Larry Bossidy, AlliedSignal's CEO was *known* for resilience. Time after time, he turned that company on a dime and gave back nine cents change when disruption hit. Yet, in the moment of that organization's greatest need for resilience (as is almost always the case in merger or divestiture), resilience stalled for one reason only: No one paid attention to the organization's mindset – its authenticity and its attitude/culture. And when they needed it most, there were no reserves left in the tank.

Apply It Right Now

Jot down the first couple of areas you can identify where the image your organization projects (how others see your organization) does not match exactly who the organization is in reality.

What The Organization Does	Why?
Eg. We don't hire the best people	...because managers don't make recruiting a priority
Eg. We don't always make it easy for the customer	...because our processes are not streamlined
Eg. We say we are completely integrated	...because we don't want to admit we're not
Eg. We restructure but nothing changes	...because we don't tackle the tough issues

1.	
2.	
3.	

Think of that last three or four major decisions made by your team or organization; perhaps it was an acquisition, or the decision to restructure or shift an approach.

Decisions:	
1.	
2.	
3.	

Now, answer the following for each decision you listed above:

- What examples can you find where the organization was being authentic?

- Where does it seem they are less so? Why?

- In your opinion, should they have been more, or less authentic? Sometimes there is a business reason for both.

- What was the prevailing attitude the organization was expressing in each decision? (For example, resignation, determination, competitiveness, reaction, victimization, etc.)

Now think of a leader you have worked for, perhaps someone involved in the decisions above. Answer the same questions for the leader (as you observed them) as you did for the organization.

What have you learned from answering these questions?

Taking It with You

- An organization's mindset is a critical component of its ability to be resilient. Mindset is made up of the organization's authenticity and attitude. Attitude, in an organizational context, has a lot to do with culture.

- An organization can get caught up in spending time managing an image it projects to the world that is different from reality. This is destructive to resilience because it shifts focus away from what matters – delivering results.

CHAPTER 14

How Comfort
Zones Hold
Organizations Hostage
(And How To Break Free)

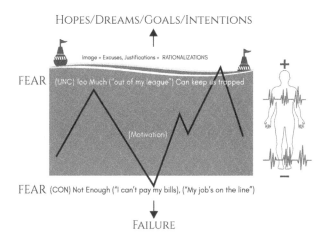

HOPES/DREAMS/GOALS/INTENTIONS

Image = Excuses, Justifications = RATIONALIZATIONS

FEAR (UNC) Too Much ("out of my league") Can keep us trapped

(Motivation)

FEAR (CON) Not Enough ("I can't pay my bills"), ("My job's on the line")

FAILURE

"Before anything great is really achieved,
your comfort zone must be disturbed."

– Ray Lewis

There is a deeper dilemma when talking about resilience as related to organizations and teams. Just as we stepped aside from the LeaderShift® Resilience Framework to examine derailers of personal resilience, we will now do the same for organizational resilience.

Some of you may be wondering why more than half of a book about building *organizational* resilience has gotten in your head and become so personal. Well, resilience *is* personal. Organizations are made up of people and people are personal. Because of that, the same rules apply, and the same thinking goes into building individual resilience as it does to strengthen organizations. It just requires a few more people to build it intentionally.

With that same thinking, come very similar types of risks that threaten to derail our ability to build resilience. The first of those is getting trapped in our comfort zone. We spent a lot of time in Part One thinking about our comfort zones. Surprise: Organizations have comfort zones, too. It is important that we recognize them, name them and call them out. We can't break free of patterns we are unaware of and organizations cannot solve problems (or take advantage of opportunities) they aren't talking about.

If an organization has a purpose that lies outside of its collective comfort zone, achieving it will require discipline and effort to recognize the boundaries of the "known zone" and to mobilize people to do something differently. That's what adaptive challenges are all about.

Can you think of something your organization has tried to do or that was (or is) outside of its comfort zone?

Here are some recent examples:

- A diverse manufacturing company, made up of a portfolio of different independently run businesses, realizes it needs to find economies of scale in a shared service model where support functions like HR, Finance and IT are centralized to serve the entire company versus being duplicated in each business unit. This organization's comfort zone is keeping support functions close to the business. Until its leaders begin to think about support functions differently, they will never find economies of scale in sharing services.

- A company in Latin America where accountants are used to yellow ruled paper and pencils with pink erasers, suddenly find themselves needing to implement enterprise financial software. Imagine training that begins with how to use a mouse! This organization's employees, to the most junior level, will need to build basic computer and software expertise to get out of their comfort zone and find any efficiency in the new system.

- A small entrepreneurial start up, bought by a Fortune 10 company, needs to integrate into the parent company, while maintaining the differentiated customer value proposition that was built through innovation and an entrepreneurial mindset. Inevitably, it's leaders and managers will need to get comfortable presenting business cases and delivering results in collaboration with the new parent company if they want to deliver comparable value.

- In a merger where two cultures are deeply embedded, the new leadership team must determine what the new organization will stand for. It is likely that aspects of the new culture will be outside the comfort zone of at least part of the organization.

- A company that viewed IT as "overhead" suddenly needs to come to terms with technology as a key driver of its new strategy to stay competitive. Building a technology strategy and relying on it to differentiate the company from its competitors will push it out of its comfort zone.

- A cost-driven, penny-counting organization realizes it needs a culture of high-touch customer service. Leaders will need to get comfortable investing in services as they have never done before in order to meet that market-driven mandate.

- A relationship-driven sales team is suddenly up against a competitor with weaker relationships, but a lot more data that is useful to its customers. The salespeople must leave their relationship-based comfort zone, embrace digital transformation, and shift their perception of how they add value if they want to keep customers with a new expectation.

Each of these is an adaptive challenge we have worked on that requires an organization to make tradeoffs in what has been valued or how they have acted in the past. Many of those tradeoffs require loss, even if it is just the loss of how they've always done something. It is only through making those tradeoffs that these organizations will be break free of their organizational comfort zones.

Organizations are pushed outside of their "known zones" every day when they face adaptive challenges. It is most important to recognize when this happens because there is only one way out: Alignment around purpose. It's the same for getting out of our own comfort zones. An organization and its leadership team MUST be in complete alignment with a clearly articulated purpose if they are to make the kinds of shifts required in today's market. They must *very quickly* be able to identify when they are approaching the boundaries of their comfort zone, so they can "double down" and focus on what they need to do to break out of it.

Apply It Right Now

Think about the organization you work in and/or lead, and then answer:

- In what kinds of situations does your company operate within its corporate comfort zone?

> *Example: A retailer in the US market was extremely comfortable operating there. When it expanded into Mexico, it was challenged to remember its purpose of global expansion as its leaders re-thought the business model and learned to do some things differently, things that Mexican customers expected.*

- Where does your company hit the top and bottom of existing comfort zones? What kinds of situations feel "uncomfortable" when the organization deals with them?

> *Example: The leadership team of a bank that had grown by acquisition needed to prove to their shareholders that they could increase synergies and reduce cost. The organization hit the top of its comfort zone when they had to trust each leader's assessment of their people and make difficult decisions on whom to keep and whom to let go.*
>
> *The same organization hit the bottom of its comfort zone when it procrastinated in finishing the integration and were in danger of not delivering results to shareholders fast enough.*

- What is the organizational purpose that will enable your company to get out of its comfort zone?

> *Example: At the bank above, their desire to continue to grow – both organically and by acquisition – and to become the number one commercial lender in their region, was the purpose that drove them to trust each other's talent decisions, and to align around a shared vision, allowing for full integration.*

Taking It with You

- Organizations have comfort zones too – patterns of behaviors, ways of thinking, and emotional norms. Some are helpful, some are not. It behooves us to identify which are which.

- Becoming aware of, recognizing, and naming the kinds of decisions or actions that push your team or organization out of its comfort zone will help build strategies for breaking free of the trap.

- Having (and knowing) the team or organization's purpose is the only sure way to break through the top end of its comfort zone.

CHAPTER 15

Two Major De-Railers To Organizational Resilience (And How To Stop Them)

"Inclusion is about creating a better world for everyone."

– Diane Richler

Resilience is an extremely personal topic and we know organizations have a better chance at becoming resilient if leaders have taken the personal initiative to intentionally build their own resilience. But how do we build the muscles required to be resilient when the organization itself is causing the need to be resilient in the first place?

In Part One, we felt so strongly about the trap of guilt and resentment, that we called them the "cancers that eat resilience alive." As we shift our thinking to building resilient organizations, there are two similar traps that, if left alone, are toxic enough to do the same thing. The ripple effect is greater because of the number of people impacted. These traps may not be what you would expect, but we see them every day, so it's time to start talking about them: They are #MeToo and food. Both impact your team's ability to bring their best and most unencumbered selves to work. Both topics are important because they have the power to make people miserable. And when people are miserable, they cannot be resilient, no matter how many frameworks you try to put in place.

It's no understatement that corporate life is tough. It is. And it often breeds the kind of stress and disruption that cause people to either need to cope—or to think ahead and build resilience. The idea, now that we have come this far, is to ensure that the team or organization we lead doesn't have to be so tough. Not on our watch, anyway.

Depending on your mindset, there are a couple of big things that can either result in quick wins for the quality of life on our teams, or completely derail any attempt to build resilience. Some of these will sound familiar. Some of them are not "ripe" yet. That means that not enough people are talking about them to get everyone nodding along in recognition, but remember, there was a time when phones in your hand and wireless streaming of digital music didn't have you nodding along either. Just because issues aren't ripe, doesn't mean they aren't important enough to pay attention to, *especially* when they threaten to derail resilience.

The First Big Derailer of Resilience: Moving from #MeToo to "What's Next"

A book about organizational resilience would not be complete without acknowledgement of this difficult topic: the #MeToo movement.

#MeToo came into focus in 2018 when a few courageous women spoke up and started a trend of posting "#MeToo" on social media to demonstrate how many women have been sexually victimized, harassed or otherwise taken advantage of simply because they were women. The number of #MeToo stories has been astounding, so much so that we now know that just about every woman has a #MeToo story. Yet, even more shocking are the missing circles where they are still afraid to post their stories—corporate America, largely, being one.

These women were rightly recognized as Time Magazine's, *Women* of the Year. From 1936-1999, this award was annually known as Time's "Man of the Year." Now, it is called, "Person of the Year." We have come a long way. Though I was mentioned nowhere in that issue of Time, it prominently graces my office wall, framed in deep gratitude that such a thing was acknowledged in my lifetime. I *personally* related to their pain.

I was 19 years old when I threw a chair across the desk and ran down eight flights of stairs to escape a professor as he tried to sexually assault me. I was 46 when I wrote about that experience, prompting a call from another woman whose roommate (clear across the country) threw that same chair at the same professor. She still couldn't talk about it.

A few years later I was offered a Mercedes to sleep with the president of a business school board I has joined as its first student representative.

My co-author was 11 years-old when she was first touched inappropriately by a family friend, and 21 years-old when she was cornered in a stairwell by a business associate and told to "put out or you'll never get another contract." She didn't put out. And she still got the contract, but it was frightening and shook her confidence.

And, those are only four of our stories; there are many, many more, many far more shocking.

There are millions of #MeToo stories out there, at least one for every woman or girl who has ever lived, every single one.

Women are coming out of the shadows, admitting they have been marginalized, harassed and pushed aside simply for being female in just about every industry. Many still won't talk about their experiences, and too many men groan in frustration believing this is one big overreaction. The story is far from over. And corporate America has been slow to respond.

Organizations will not be able to build the resilience required to sustain momentum if one gender is marginalized, even occasionally, and the other is indignant—or ignorant. This kind of frustration flies in the face of productive collaboration. And the energy required to face this is siphoned from the tank of energy that could be spent on building agility and sustainable results.

The only solution that can possibly allow us to move past #MeToo will be a clear focus on "What's Next" and how we can get there *together*.

Many rejoiced when the shadows dimmed, when women came out and formed a movement that said, *"Enough is enough!"* Many women still feel that corporate America has not done nearly enough to undo the damage and create a safe environment. But this dialog cannot move forward if it remains solely about women.

Because it happens to men, too, and minorities, and others, all the time.

Men: Victimized or Indignant?

Stories of male abuse, at the hands of other men or by women, and some who have been falsely accused and labeled, continues to be an ongoing shame in our society. The recent revelations of abuse of children at the hands of Roman Catholic priests throughout the world, with thousands of known victims, underscores the obvious: The problem is chronic and wide-spread.

These kinds of incidents cause shame that undermines effectiveness. Shame is real. It is toxic. And it inhibits any attempt at building resilience, individually and on a corporate level.

✶ ✶ ✶ ✶ ✶

A male friend is a CEO who was sexually abused as a child. He is wiser now with enough experience on the other side of his story to have good instincts, a strong moral compass, and core beliefs that support him. Yet, after numerous attempts to process it, therapy included, he remains in fear that his experience will cause him to miss a cue or do something wrong, personally or professionally.

Even as an accomplished adult, he second-guesses himself constantly, a common effect of abuse. You wouldn't know it from the confidence he projects and the coping mechanisms he has built, but the shame and disorientation he carries inside have impacted his entire life. He is very successful and yet, as the shadows of his past still hound him, how many people around him will be affected, intentionally or not?

"Shame corrodes the very part of us that believes we are capable of change."

– Brene Brown

We may never know that there is someone on our team with a similar experience. We may never know whose life has been forever altered in ways that will shape their interactions, our teams, or our companies.

How many other people of every gender are out there struggling to rise above similar issues? And, how many will never acknowledge a movement because they are, by design, excluded from it? Once abuse embeds its hooks into your psyche it is there, in varying degrees, forever.

"What's Next"

Sadly, abusive experiences and horrific stories are a part of life. It is not our responsibility as leaders to fix the past, but it *is* our responsibility to acknowledge that everyone has a story and we cannot always know (or need to know) what that is. It is our responsibility to keep communication lines open and engage those people anyway. It is the work of a leader to create inclusive, engaging and safe environments where people of all kinds can to do their best work, do more with what they have, minimize the cost of distraction, and build the resilience required to optimize our resources. That is the only way to we get to "What's Next."

Resilience makes business sense

The problem with talking about sexual harassment, traditionally against women, is that sexuality does not have a monopoly on harassment and neither do women. It is perhaps even less safe to discuss the men who have been abused, many of them as children. For them, the shame can often be even greater. Many men, as well as many women, are not safe yet. That's real. "What's Next" cannot happen until they are. Until these intolerable issues of power are brought out in the open in a safe space, open to all ideologies and races, where judgment is absent and understanding and empathy are the norms, we will neither have safe workplaces nor resilient companies.

It is naïve to compare pain based on gender.

Injustice is injustice, no matter where it occurs or to whom.

And you know the indignant men. You may be one of them. They are friends, husbands, boyfriends, brothers and lovers.

They are the brave individuals who do not understand, not because they are men, but because they cannot imagine marginalizing a woman or treating her as a sexual object. Those good men are out there, and the dialogue for them is as much about being falsely accused as it is about deeds, intentional or not, that never should have happened. There are male leaders who are now afraid of meeting one-on-one with female direct reports, just "in case." To ignore these men is to miss the point, that men and women must support each other, not *despite* who we are, but because of it.

Harassment, since the dawn of time, does not ignore any gender, race or social class. And included in this dialogue must be a chance to move forward, *intentionally* building resilience in a way that unravels the tough issues, the ones that hinder personal and corporate potential. Intentionally calling out each other in a way that creates a constructive conversation is a must, one that drives learning for both sides and engages all of us in a future solidified by our resilience, not threatened by the internal politics that erode it.

Attraction

Physical attraction. Love. Chemistry. One-sided lust. It is the stuff we don't talk about that rears its head in organizations, sometimes inappropriately when it boils over. It happens, whether we like it or not, on the street, in a club, or in the office. It is a part of life, despite many, many attempts to deny or dance around it. Some are better about dealing with it than others, but physical attraction *can* be handled in ways that do not result in marginalizing or making either side uncomfortable at the office (or anywhere else, really).

So, what is the right way to handle physical attraction at work?

Is it a moral code that eliminates the gray area? Perhaps religious doctrine might dictate that. But not everyone adheres to a religious code. Based on our filters, we know that everyone comes to the table with different expectations for what "good" looks like: a good boss, good team player, good employee, good relationship, good partner, etc. Our differing perspectives do not make one right and another wrong. Instead, they create a gray space.

It may take some focus, perhaps a bit less selfishness and a bit more consideration, but respect for each other can trump the discomfort that so often comes of physical attraction.

A few ideas to do this include:

- Assume positive intent

- Ask

- Be honest

- Be an adult

- Treat the other person as an equal

And if you're still stuck, here's a suggestion: What if we all refused to say anything we wouldn't say in front of our grandmothers, or the grandmother we imagine on our best day?

Trust is Crucial

Many years ago, I moved to the majority minority (more black than white citizens) city of Memphis. My excitement about the diversity and what I might learn from it faded when a legitimately poor performer who was about to be fired accused me of racism and harassment. The feelings of helplessness, the constant second-guessing and, "what ifs," rattled my confidence to the core. The stress and humiliation of the investigation, largely exacerbated by a boss who thrived on drama, is still with me today.

My team—and many prior employees of all races—defended me behind closed doors without me throughout a six-week investigation (that felt like six years), during which I was not permitted to discuss the event. In the end, the investigation turned up exactly one fact: I had done nothing wrong. So, imagine my utter shock and dismay when, instead of supporting me, my boss then asked what I had done to my team to force them to speak up for me. How many of us (men, it's your turn) have been through something similar?

Over a decade later, those wounds are still raw.

These kinds of experiences eat away at us all. They undermine trust and they can destroy organizations. To thrive in the face of rapid, disruptive change, these situations cannot be tolerated. Sadly, in our line of work, we (the authors), have heard these stories over and over again. In the end, they are about power and how it is used.

Abuse of power kills resilience every time.

Another Big Derailer of Resilience: Food

Yes. Food. This may seem out of place, but alas, it's not something the publisher stuck in the wrong book. Perhaps ahead of its time, but disregarding dietary requirements is becoming a major derailer of resilience.

Adaptive Leadership (and #MeToo) is about *inclusion*. It's about enabling people to feel safe so that they can show up as their best selves every day at work. It's about ensuring that the static and distractions created when people are marginalized don't suck the life out of our organizations. And, it's about equipping organizations to become truly resilient by ensuring that the people in them don't need to think about anything but contributing their very best, at least at work.

Inclusion is not just about women, or men, or minorities. It's not relegated to the LGBTQ community. It's about everything, including food.

We eat at work. We eat socially. As a society, we *connect* over food. It's a huge part of our collective psyche and well-being—until it isn't.

There are an increasing number of people who either by choice or medical necessity abide by a restrictive diet. One of the most difficult parts of any restrictive diet is the *social* aspect of it. For those people, eating out, even at work, can become extremely difficult. It is difficult not only because of the lack of understanding and necessary options available, but because it opens the door to criticism, questions, and suddenly the need to explain and justify, which can hijack the flavor of a positive dining experience.

The pain hit me without warning. Over the next six months, I balanced business travel and meetings with hospital visits and painkillers to deal with debilitating abdominal pain. The specialists could not tell me why my abdomen was inflamed, and I knew that treating the pain that doubled me over, would only buy so much time. And I spend most of my life speaking in front of senior leaders. Frankly, I didn't think I was resilient enough to go on, and I sure wasn't energized or elevated.

Worst was that I pride myself on being "low maintenance" to my clients. I make very few special requests, I stay wherever the client puts me, and I carry what I need. But now, I couldn't eat. It didn't take long to realize that my focus on secretly finding safe food without asking for it was taking over my ability to be effective.

I considered leaving the successful consulting business I founded because I couldn't eat what clients were serving and I didn't want to be the one who had to ask about the menu in advance.

Finally, an incredibly persistent doctor figured out that my body does not digest fructose. Fructose is the natural sugar that occurs in fruits and vegetables. It also hides in ingredients in just about anything processed or served in a packaged sauce. As soon as I stopped eating it, the pain stopped. At the time, I had stopped traveling. The thought of attempting to leave overnight when most restaurants and meetings don't have anything safe for me to eat, stopped me in my tracks.

There are people going through issues like this in every organization in the world. Think of those with peanut allergies. Believe me, it is terrifying.

Many of us, through medical necessity, are thrust into situations like this with no choice or preparation. Any new celiac, allergy, intolerance or malabsorption patient, at some point, will suddenly find themselves in a situation where it is no longer safe to just sit down and enjoy a meal. Instead, they must first figure out the ingredients of anything they expect to eat. Often, things like gluten, lactose or fructose are not easily understood by restaurant staff and the employee, trying desperately not to be singled out, must decipher what is least likely to give them a reaction from a list of available options, hoping against hope that the guess they or the wait staff made works in their favor.

As if that isn't challenging and stressful enough for those with a serious medical condition, add a few laughs, eye rolls, and comments muttered from colleagues. Where does the focus shift to at that point? It shifts *off* what's important. It shifts *away* from any results to be delivered or productive relationships with your team and *onto* being self-conscious and uncomfortable—back down the hierarchy of needs to safety. No one can contribute their best when under stress.

Organizations cannot build resilience when people are marginalized, regardless of the reason. And the way we handle food, believe it or not, has become an increasingly big one.

In my case, fortunately, I had a purpose. My comfort zone had me trapped secretly foraging for food but that wasn't the purpose I was after. I found a way out because of my own Resilience Framework. No diet is impossible, I'm pretty creative and I can now talk about it and ask for help.

There isn't a person alive who makes a lifestyle choice as significant as a diet for any reason other than to improve their health or support a deeply-held conviction.

That is a person's right, and often it's their *necessity*. We don't always know someone's reason or story and frankly, it is none of our business. If leaders and organizations want to become resilient, supporting employee's food choices, either with options or inclusion, is crucial. It creates safety and inclusion and allows us to bring their unbridled best self to work.

Any judgment or lack of support on these types of choices, inhibits resilience. As leaders and colleagues, we don't need to understand what those issues may be, but we need to support them. That is, IF we want to remove the barriers to resilience.

Wrapping it Up

Imagine a world where, instead of aligning around a set of principles (biblical, religious code or any sort of black-and-white rules), we focus in on *how* power is used.

Power can be used to intimidate or inspire. On its best and most adaptive day, power can be used to mobilize and engage people in dialogue that drives learning for all parties. It can be used to drive a healthy organizational dynamic that supports a collaborative exchange of ideas and eliminates distractions and static caused by internal "politics" and the need for personal agendas. Anything that is not in support of that purpose is either a misuse, abuse, or a lost opportunity to use power for its highest good.

The muck that sticks to us after some of these situations, regardless of where power might have been abused, can cause us to second-guess ourselves, and the "what ifs" threaten our ability to be authentic because the things we know deep inside to be true, suddenly aren't what they seem to be.

The best antidote is to create an environment conducive to talking, one dedicated to creating transparent, connected conversations that create understanding and ferret out common ground.

This is the very same environment required for *Adaptive Leadership* and the very same environment that nurtures ideas. It is an environment and a filter that does not judge, but instead, seeks to engage and understand others. It is an environment that understands that good ideas are found and built upon by every level, every gender and every affinity. And it lets them flow unhindered.

Everyone deserves to work in a safe environment. That's good for business; it raises productivity and propels profits.

Most important, it makes us and our teams resilient.

> *"The more you understand the human condition, the better you are as a business person. Human depth makes business sense."*
>
> – Peter Koestenbaum

Making it Stick

Many people have a story that changed them forever and altered the way they view life.

It is vital to remember that who we are as people shapes who we become as leaders. Our filters and past experiences define much of how we lead and participate on a team. No matter how hard we may try to suppress or ignore the effects of our stories, shame and anger shape our lenses in ways that are less than productive. Unresolved emotions resulting from life-altering events detract from the contributions we might make, as well as the influence we have on others and the contributions we might make through them. The effect is exponential and is best faced head-on.

For those who have not done the work of processing and releasing past traumas of any kind—marginalization, humiliation, or hurts—here are a few thoughts and resources to consider. Not all will apply to everyone, and these are *suggestions* only, but it is by acknowledging, processing and releasing the residue caused by destructive events that people are able to intentionally quiet the disruption those past hurts cause.

- Consider therapy or coaching of some kind. Get recommendations, interview a few therapists/coaches and choose someone with whom you feel safe to be yourself. If you had a therapist in the past and "got nothing out of it" you either picked the wrong therapist or put nothing into the process. Try again.

- If you're all talked out but still exhibiting counter-productive behavioral patterns, consider something like **EMDR** (**Eye Movement Desensitization and Reprocessing,** an integrative psychotherapy approach effective for the treatment of trauma) that does not require talking about your feelings to help your brain make connections faster and come out on the other side.

- Consider NLP (**Neuro Linguistic Programming**) which is very effective in overcoming negative emotions regarding an event, or fear.

- Consider attending **The Trust Program™**, put on by Cynthia Barlow and C3 Conversations. This is, quite literally, a life-altering retreat that accelerates your ability to trust yourself and life in general, as well as remove some of the self-doubt inherent in living.

- **Know that you are not alone.** *Everyone* has a story that would break your heart in two if you heard them tell it. We have. Thousands of time. Abuse need not be sexual to carry crippling long-term costs. We *all* have bruises. Every intimidating "big boy" I've ever coached is, somewhere inside, a wounded child. That's why he lashes out. Like a wounded animal, he's simply scared.

- Know that whatever it was, you can find your way back, and simply *trying*, admitting it, though scary as hell when you start, is an act of courage that permeates your being and shows up at the office. **Trying is worth the effort.** Because *you* are worth the effort—and so are the people you live with or lead.

- **Start a conversation** with your team. Sometimes, that's all it takes.

Taking it With You

- Everyone has a story that will break your heart. Remember that the next time you think something nasty about someone you feel you have to "tolerate." Exercise your empathy muscles.

- We cannot create safe work environments without first addressing issues of injustice, harassment and marginalization, regardless of gender.

- It is our responsibility as leaders to acknowledge those situations when they occur, address them head-on, and open the door for constructive conversations.

- These kinds of conversations, and the environments that encourage them, are critical to building resilient organizations.

- Safety inclusive environments can be created in everything that differentiates people, including food choices.

- Resilience cannot exist without trust. It's a simple equation. No safety, no trust. No trust, no authentic engagement. No engagement, no business—at least, not long-term.

CHAPTER 16

Choices That Drive Resilience And Build Trust

Resilience IS A RESULT OF:

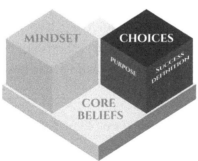

*"Trust is the glue of life. It's the most
essential ingredient in effective communication."*

– Steven Covey

The second component of the Leader*Shift*® Resilience Framework is about the choices we make. Similar to the way in which we looked at Mindset, we want to take what we learned in Part One (focused on individual resilience) about how we make choices and apply it now to organizations.

The notion that we frequently make unconscious choices based on blockages and payoffs applies to organizations as well, perhaps even more so, because a group can create a groundswell of momentum when it binds together. Adaptive challenges frequently cause a group to rally together against a change. This resistance is a primary reason why a 1994 research study still holds true today: A full 70% of organizational change projects fail to achieve the results they intend.

When facing an adaptive challenge, an organization that is not aligned, or has not built resilience, will do anything it can to maintain the status quo. Group-think is powerful and the magnetic forces pulling towards the status quo can defy logic and reason in the quest to avoid the work required to create real change.

Organizations often use work avoidance as a payoff whether they consciously realize it or not. Often companies face major adaptive challenges, yet instead of doing the difficult and complex work of solving them, they do *anything* else.

A major retailer needed to reorganize and streamline its stores' organization. They had a great reputation for customer service and had over-staffed and over-hired experts with specialized skills because of it. When sales went down, they could not make the numbers work. All those people are expensive, and in a lot of cases unnecessary, as not every customer needed that level of service. The company needed to find creative ways of serving customers with less cost.

The adaptive challenge they underestimated was that customer service was a core value of the organization. No one–not one leader–was willing to make the tough call and reduce the service level. So, they brought in a consultant with a fancy suit to do it for them.

The consulting firm brought in a small army of junior people and spent six months doing analytics to justify the decision. They left the retailer with a binder full of recommendations for how to save money.

How many of those recommendations were implemented? Not one.

We got the call a year later when the stakes were a bit higher – the issue had "ripened" – and the leaders were finally ready to make some tough decisions that had little to do with what was in those binders.

How often do struggling organizations shift everyone's focus to cost-cutting when sales are down? What if the same amount of effort were put into the more difficult work of driving revenue? We know in our heads that we can't save our way to prosperity, yet because the technical work of cost cutting is easier and more comfortable, we often prioritize it above the more difficult work of innovation, creating a "blue ocean" (a space where there is minimal competition and we can differentiate our organization) or finding new revenue streams.

We *need to* figure out how to drive top-line growth, but instead, we avoid it.

If every ineffective behavior has a payoff, what is the organizational payoff for work avoidance?

Well, first, we get to stay safely inside our comfort zone. No one has to think too far outside of the proverbial box. We don't have to rethink anything, *and* we get to feel good about having accomplished something. The cost is the false sense of accomplishment, because eventually you cannot cut enough to stay in business or keep shareholders happy. But boy do we make heroes out of people who find savings!

Is that to say that finding savings is a bad thing? No—unless it is taking time and pulling the organization away from unraveling real issues that hinder progress. There is, however, a hidden cost of work avoidance: The organization never builds the confidence that comes from knowing that they mobilize to solve adaptive challenges.

There are all kinds of things organizations do, both consciously and unconsciously that come under the heading of work avoidance. Placing a disproportionate amount of effort on technical components of broader adaptive challenge is a great example. We've worked with several large companies who have implemented sophisticated performance management systems in a quest to improve the way they manage employee performance. They have spent months implementing and delivering training on a complex system, while completely disregarding the fact that the single greatest driver of effective performance management is the quality of the dialog an employee has with their manager. The focus remains on *how to use a system* when it needs to be on *how to have better conversations.*

Certainly, none of those organizations were *consciously* trying to avoid work. Their choices, in fact, created a lot of unnecessary work. What they *didn't* do was mobilize people to do the real work necessary to solve the problem. Instead, they used up a disproportionate amount of reserves in the tank that could have been used for something else.

Work avoidance wastes resources that could be used to solve real issues and it kills resilience.

Wrapping It Up

We need to direct our attention toward making choices that benefit the long-term strategy of the organization.

When we make choices as an organization, particularly if we are trying to build resilience, we must think carefully about the costs and payoffs inherent in our decisions. That way, we can ensure that they are *consciously* aligned with our purpose and definition of success.

Making intentional choices builds trust between companies and clients, and between leaders and their teams. And trust is an integral ingredient in the resilience recipe.

Making it Stick

List a couple of adaptive challenges your organization has faced and some of the decisions that came about as a result of them. These can be things you were involved in, or that were made by others. For each challenge:

- What components of the challenge were adaptive?

- What decisions were made?

- Did the decision address the adaptive work?

- Were any decisions made unconsciously?

- What were some of the payoffs and benefits of the decisions that were made?

Taking It with You

- Organizations make unconscious choices based on blockages and payoffs just as people do. Work avoidance is one such example.

- An organization that is not aligned or has not built resilience will do whatever it can to maintain the status quo. Group-think is powerful: Avoidance in action.

- Work avoidance wastes resources and kills resilience.

- Trustworthiness is the glue, the foundation, of all successful, resilient people—and organizations.

- Making intentional choices with a long-term focus, rather than the short-term expedient choice, builds that trust.

CHAPTER 17

How Your Purpose, Definition Of Success & Core Beliefs Drive Alignment

"An organization without purpose manages human resources, whereas an organization with purpose mobilizes people."

– Juan Carlos Eichholz

G etting clear on a purpose, a definition of success and a set of core beliefs might be simpler (or at least more obvious) for organizations than it is for individuals. An organization is formed with a purpose in mind and while that may get clouded by mergers, acquisitions, or changes in the competitive landscape, it usually has something to do with the contribution the team or organization makes within the corporate realm. In an organizational context, these things are frequently disguised as a mission, vision and values (or principles). The semantics of what you call them is not important; alignment around them is the critical aspect that drives resilience.

Know the Purpose & Define Success

The degree to which our teams are clear on the purpose and mission of the organization fundamentally impacts their ability to be resilient. This is not about memorizing a hollow statement posted on a wall in a conference room. This is about every single team member being able to articulate, in their own words, the purpose of the organization (or the purpose of what they are working on) and what a successful outcome looks like. When the chips are down and we need all the reserves we can harness to deal with disruption, energy expended on debating about the goal actually reduces our ability to achieve it. It's that simple.

Purpose can also be used to guide our actions in a particular situation. This is just as important as the organization's purpose, since clarifying the purpose of each situation we walk into will equip us to walk out having made decisions aligned with that purpose.

Knowing what success looks like works the same way. Begin with the end in mind. Anyone who has negotiated with a union or a works council knows you don't enter that situation without a goal and a plan in mind. Imagine the power of thinking through the decisions we'll be called to make in difficult situations, *before* we enter them, from a purpose-driven, success-delineated perspective.

I flew to Europe with a goal everyone said was impossible.

The head of Labor Relations at a very large global consumer products company had created a labor negotiation strategy in the US that had saved millions of dollars and the company wanted to do the same thing in Europe.

Europe, where the labor landscape is different everywhere you turn; where every country has different work councils with different philosophies, cultures and laws; where every country's corporate president had a specific agenda and profit and loss. Europe, where they were tired of being bossed around by the American headquarters.

I had a better chance of herding a colony of feral cats to the top of Everest than gaining consensus in Europe.

I boarded the plane uncertain that all the stakeholders would even show up for the meeting; two had refused my invitation and told me I was crazy to even ask them to sit down together. There was no mandate from the CEO and 5,000 years of European history still dictated which country teams would work together.

My boss and I had an impossibly crazy idea. And my global credibility depended on my ability to pull it off. It was the kind of meeting that demanded an ace up my sleeve–which I had.

In conversation, and by written survey, every single one of the stakeholders involved had told me that it would create efficiency and save money if they all approached labor negotiations the same way, leaning in the same direction when faced with a choice. Of course, all of them had different ideas of what that looked like, but they all agreed in private that it was a good idea.

We had, at least behind closed doors, a mutual purpose.

Never have I prepared more. We ran every scenario we could think of, prepared for every objection and built a solid business case. We did anticipate the fight that broke out or the stalemate when representatives from each country told us they agreed with us but would not support the idea publicly or convince their country President to go along with it. The meeting stalled. We were stuck. We took a break.

Returning to the room, I realized that united, we had a purpose – a cause worth millions. I threw away the agenda we had spent days preparing as my boss sat back in his chair, wringing his hands. I asked the group one question.

"What would it take to sell this to your team?"

The French Vice-President, who had been silent and a bit uncomfortable with English, began to speak. He told us how his leader needed to save face and how it needed to be his idea. We strategized and turned everyone's focus to how we could package the idea to sell it in France. Then Great Britain. Then Holland. Then Germany.

Because of a clear organizational purpose, we turned the impossible into reality: One global labor strategy. We were the first company of its kind to pull that off.

Knowing our purpose enabled us to switch gears in mid-flight. It empowered us to focus on results when even a well-crafted plan didn't work.

Juan Carlos Eichholz, adaptive leadership expert and author of *Adaptive Capacity: How Organizations Thrive in a Changing World*, calls an organization's purpose, its "soul." He believes that work is not only about doing well, but also about having a lasting and positive impact on the world. "For this reason, an organization without a purpose will not be able to attract people who work with purpose." Eichholz describes an organization without a purpose as *industrial* and focused exclusively on performing tasks *efficiently*. Where an organization with purpose will go beyond the task in realizing its full potential [and the potential of the people within it].

Core Beliefs

As we work through the framework with clients, we know that core beliefs are the element on which all else rests. We cover them last, but they are the foundation. Just like resilient individuals, organizations also find it difficult to stand up when they are not clear about what they stand *on*.

In organizations, core beliefs are often called values or principles. No matter the terminology, the important thing is how they are created and what they really reflect. Core beliefs must pass the snicker test to make any contribution to resilience. This has a lot to do with how they were created and who created them. Doing this collaboratively to create alignment is absolutely necessary.

Espoused values or principles are the ones we *say* we have. Most organizations have an artifact on a wall somewhere that says they value excellence, integrity, teamwork, etc. As a general rule, few people pay attention to the list because they sound like "motherhood and apple pie" and they may or may not reflect what really happens day to day.

An organization's true core beliefs are the values people actually *use*, those they see demonstrated, the ones that guide behaviors and difficult decisions. If we can get *those* values on the wall or get leaders to role model the ones that are up there every day, they will contribute to resilience. The Johnson and Johnson Credo is a great example of this. So is the AutoZone Pledge or J.M. Huber's Principles. I don't think I've ever sat in a meeting at any of those places where someone didn't refer back to one of those artifacts.

A prior client was the first non-family CEO of a diverse, family-owned, portfolio manufacturing company. When he took over a decade ago, the company was not in a position to spend extra money.

There was a lot of pressure on Joe (not his real name), not only to steer the company through a slow economic period, but also to exhibit leadership as a new CEO with a vastly different style from that of the prior leader.

Shortly after Joe took the helm, there was a tragic accident resulting in a fatality in one of the organization's manufacturing facilities. In his analysis of the situation, Joe learned that there was a piece of equipment that could make the manufacturing process safer and prevent future accidents like this one.

This equipment represented a $10MM expense at a time when the company was financially strapped, but Joe didn't think twice about it. He didn't need to. One of this company's foundational principles was world-class safety. Joe saw to it that the company sacrificed other initiatives, found the money and purchased the equipment.

Wrapping It Up

To contribute to resilience, organizational core beliefs cannot simply hang on a wall, they MUST be used in real life, in the heat of the moment when it matters most. When we build routines that set expectations that our core beliefs will guide our actions, we operate with confidence; decisions will be made that adhere to those beliefs and values, even when we are not in the room.

When the tank gets empty, when we are focused on something else and most need resilience, the sheer power of this becomes evident. We save time and energy by reducing debate and moving ahead delivering our purpose, as we intended to do.

A clear purpose, definition of success and organizational core beliefs or values operates like the GPS on a cell phone: Pointing the way. When those things are real, they are ever-present, directing us to the desired destination, even as they streamline and enable difficult decisions.

Making It Stick

Corporate Purpose

Answer the following questions as honestly as you can

- What are some of the documents your organization uses to broadly define its purpose?

- Are they clear, mutually understood, and agreed upon?

- In your own words, what is the purpose of your company?

- What do you see the company doing to live out its purpose? How is it demonstrated?

- Do you see any areas where it is NOT acting in accordance with its purpose? Elaborate.

How Does Your Organization Define Success?

Answer the following about your team or the organization you lead:

- What do successful people do there? What is rewarded? And how?

- What does the organization count as a "win"?

- Make a list of 5-10 things that define success for your organization

Understanding the Organization's Core Beliefs

Spend some time gathering what documents and artifacts you can find published by your organization. Look for things like annual reports, vision/mission statements, values, goals and objectives. Answer the following:

- What do these things have in common?

- What message do they send to those who read them?

- How well are they used to drive decisions?

- Think of a decision your team or leader made recently. What components of the organization's core beliefs were considered?

- Do you believe the organization is in alignment with its stated core beliefs?

- If not, draft a set of the real core beliefs – things that you know to be true and valued by the organization.

Taking it With You

- The degree to which teams are clear on the purpose and mission of an organization fundamentally impacts the team's ability to be resilient.

- Know what success looks like: Begin with the end in mind.

- In organizations, core beliefs are usually called values or principles. What's important is how they are created and whether they reflect reality.

- These three–determining a clear purpose, a definition of success and a clearly adhered to set of core beliefs–enables organizations to streamline difficult decisions.

CHAPTER 18:

Where To Go
From Here

"If you're not evolving, you're dying."

– Marcus Lemonis

When we were young, there was no challenge too daunting. We believed in ourselves. We believed in the world around us, and we ran with the wind at our backs, hair flying. We were unstoppable. But somewhere along the way, life happened. For many of us, it was corporate life. A few disappointments, maybe some real trauma. We were beat up a few times. We got up and we fell again. And early on, maybe we ran with a limp, but we ran. And then some of us slowed down. A few even stopped running completely.

Building Resilience is about finding that unstoppable spirit again. It's about picking up your unstoppability and running with it—and inspiring your team to run alongside you.

The spirit of resilience is like the American dream, the hope of entrepreneurship, and a bag of popcorn all at the same time. It's a Coke on a hot day when you pop the top and know that little jolt of caffeine and refreshment will give you what you need to finish building the project. Because in this life, we're darn sure going to need it.

Building resilience for you or your team
means building a life well lived.

Resilience is worth it.

And more important, it's worth it for your team. Resilience improves the quality of life in organizations by reducing stress and equipping teams and organizations to address and overcome adaptive challenges. Building it can be an enormously empowering exercise.

Back in the nineties, a brand new, young consultant walked into a large reengineering project at a general hospital New Jersey. It was one of those crazy projects with a 30% cost savings goal, where the whole place is running around fearful that they might lose their jobs.

At the time all the consultant could think about was how long it would take before they'd figure out she had no idea what she was doing or how she could help them. She was assigned the pieces of the project that she would be responsible for and asked what resources she needed. She jokingly replied, "the toughest clients you've got." They gave her a team of seasoned unionized nurses. The joke was over. Most of them had 30-40 years with the hospital. They were scared, cynical, angry, and tired of someone trying to tell them a better way to do their job. Now they had a 24- year old to contend with.

The consultant asked a lot of questions and figured out fast that those experienced employees knew exactly what needed to be done to fix the problems in the hospital, but they were beat up, exhausted and had been ignored for years. Their tanks were on empty.

She thought long and hard and came to them with an idea. Without even asking her boss, she asked if they thought they could create a profit center and generate 30% more revenue. It turned out the nurses had written a plan to do just that a few years prior, but no one had listened.

Instead of researching and developing recommendations, that young consultant worked with the nurses to create alignment around what the organization could be on its best day. Soon, the team found a pulse – a renewed energy. They built a business case that included a passionate appeal to what the organization stood for in the community, authentic to its history. Six months later, the team's recommendations were approved by the board.

Out of nearly 100 teams created to complete reengineer an entire hospital, those recommendations were the only revenue-generating ones presented.

Three years later, they were the only recommendations implemented that were still in place in the organization.

I was that young consultant and the work accomplished there proved to me that it was possible to make life easier in corporations.

✳ ✳ ✳ ✳ ✳

When I think back on why I do this work, that project was the beginning. Before it was even an idea, the Leader*Shift*® Resilience Framework was used to help a team mobilize to solve an adaptive challenge. They created a resilient mindset that was authentic and seriously adjusted their attitude. They made recommendations in keeping with a clear purpose and definition of success. The core belief we shared was that it was possible that no one lose their job on our watch. And no one did.

We Can't Solve What We Aren't Talking About

The nurses were disengaged and had been for a long time. Early in the project, they gave me a formal "Award of Valor" for bringing them back to the table long after the organization's leadership had forgotten about them.

> *"The biggest concern for any organization should be when its most passionate people become quiet."*
>
> – Tim McClure

When we face adaptive challenges and need to build resilient teams, what matters most is getting issues on the table, where we can deal with them. It is the only way to create alignment.

Since resilient organizations are made up of resilient people who are *intentional* about building the core competencies that comprise resilience in *themselves*, it is important to put issues on the table, to talk about them, and to prepare for challenges *before* they arise. This is not the same thing as "risk management;" that's far too intellectual an approach.

Resilience is emotionally driven. And emotions are messy. But the more we try to ignore, marginalize, or explain them away, the more they take on increasing power. Eventually, our unexamined motivations start calling the shots in difficult situations and conversations, like the Wizard of Oz pulling levers from behind a curtain.

There Is More at Stake Than Survival

Right now, in today's world of rapid, disruptive change, resilience is a required prerequisite for survival, and more, for a fulfilling life, at home or at work. But, developing it is a learned skill, a practiced art.

Resilience requires a framework for understanding and developing it. The authors have attempted to present a cogent case for such a framework.

We believe this framework can be implemented everywhere, but despite its simplicity, we know from personal experience that doing so is far from easy. Creating alignment and having the discipline to stay in the game when things get tough on a team is rarely easy.

Here's the Bottom Line:

The ability to bounce back from setbacks better, stronger and wiser—to become *truly resilient*—is based on our willingness to look behind the curtain of our intentions, to drill down to our core values, to confront our attitudes and biases, to clarify our purpose and to define for ourselves what success looks and feels like.

And we need to do this as individuals as well as for our organizations in order to do more than simply survive. We want to be energized and elevated. We want to thrive.

Without that willingness and determination to exercise self-reflection, becoming a resilient individual or developing a resilient organization remains outside our grasp.

With it, all things become possible.

We Can Help

The authors of this book have been working with organizations to create alignment and build resilience for years. We've worked with hundreds of clients across almost every industry and size. But that isn't where we started. We know your pain because we have been there, in your shoes as leaders in organizations too.

If you would like some assistance in creating a Resilience Framework for your organization, even if only for a piece of it, we invite you to reach out to us. We are always eager to share our ideas, conduct a Resilience Workshop, or help your organization create alignment.

And We Do It With You

Our own core beliefs include the importance of doing things *with* you, not *to* you. We don't take up space in conference rooms, bring in a huge team or wander your halls talking to your boss about you. There are no armies of junior people and you're not likely to get a binder. Just results.

While we've adopted a filter that "life is hard," it doesn't mean that we can't help make it easier for you and your organization. That is why we do this work.

Feel Free To Contact Us Directly:

Cynthia Barlow   Jennifer Eggers

cynthia@c3conversations.com   jeggers@leadershiftinsights.com

Our Ask

If you enjoyed reading *Resilience: It's Not About Bouncing Back* and found it helpful, we'd surely appreciate hearing your thoughts and an honest review.

Author's Note: Jennifer Eggers

I was a sickly kid, certainly not athletic. I hated cold water and never quite understood the notion of jumping in. Then two things happened. I took a job after college working for Arthur Andersen in New York City, an office with one of the roughest cultures in the world. I was the first consultant they had ever hired without a master's degree and ironically, while I didn't qualify for the appropriate training without a masters, I was expected to lead client engagements as if I had. I jumped in. It damn near killed me to figure it out and not let anyone see me sweat, but I did it. Three short years later, I was up for an early promotion to manager when I left Arthur Andersen. The second thing that happened was someone at the lake I lived on threw me a ski rope.

Two consulting businesses, three state waterski championships, one top fifty national ranking (Women's Slalom), nine senior leadership roles, five cities, four houses, two car accidents, three life-threatening illnesses, one car fire, a brush with losing everything, thousands of clients, and one bluegrass band later, I asked a friend, "What is the story only I can tell?" "Resilience," he said. "Jennifer, you are nothing if not resilient. How do you keep coming back?"

As I sought to figure that out, I realized two things were true:

First, when God is all you have, He is all you need. Period.

Second, both the characteristics of resilient people AND the way individuals build resilience are exactly the same for organizations. Resilience can be built. It can be learned. It is essential for leadership, particularly the kind of adaptive leadership required for the pace of change and disruption the world is facing. Because of Cynthia Barlow, I knew how to do that. And it has nothing to do with bouncing back.

These two realizations have shaped both my life and that of our company, Leader*Shift* Insights®.

With this book, it is my hope to make corporate life better by reaching those who would like help creating alignment or have not attended our Resilience Workshop. If you like the book or would like to learn more, Cynthia and I welcome your thoughts, feedback and, of course, a great review.

If you would like to talk about how you can create alignment in your organization or put your leaders through a Resilience Workshop to increase your organization's resilience in the face of rapid, disruptive change, call us. It's what we do.

Please visit our website at www.leadershiftinsights.com, subscribe to our blog, and follow us on social media at:

Facebook.com/leadershiftinsights
Facebook.com/jennifereggersspeaker
Linkedin.com/in/eggers
@JenniferEggers

Jennifer Eggers, CSP
Atlanta, Georgia

Jennifer is the Founder and President at Leader*Shift* Insights®, an organization alignment firm focused on aligning structure, people, and investments to drive strategy and thrive in the face of change. A consultant, coach and speaker, her passion is getting people on the same page, building resilience and equipping leaders to do more with what they already have – in the field or in the board room. Jennifer has an early operational background and bias for execution. A masterful facilitator, she is adept at assessing the big picture, getting to the heart of issues, creating shared agendas, engaging diverse stakeholders and unraveling tough issues that hinder results.

Jennifer's integrated approach to developing leaders and organizations, optimizing talent and succession, structure and processes enables transformation, learning and productive dialog. She is the creator of RapidOD, the collaborative and fast approach to restructuring; and highly popular workshops on Influence, Resilience and Driving Sustainable Change.

In over 20 years, Jennifer has coached entire leadership teams as well as leaders of many Fortune 500 companies. She is known for repositioning personal brands, driving behavior change and equipping leaders to drive exponential performance through others. Jennifer is an advanced practitioner in Adaptive Leadership and a member of the Adaptive Leadership Network.

Jennifer is a former Partner with Cambridge Leadership Group, Vice-President, Leadership Development & Learning for Bank of America, and has held several other senior roles in Learning, Organization & Leadership Development at AutoZone and Coca-Cola Enterprises. She has designed and executed large-scale initiatives across the globe, including mergers, enterprise restructuring, talent management, performance management and team development. Her "kitchen English" approach and proprietary, research-backed solutions resonate equally well on the shop floor as they do facilitating complex strategy and issues resolution sessions in the C-Suite.

She is a former nationally ranked water-skier, bumbling bluegrass musician, and is owned by a Devon Rex and a Peterbald cat. She has a reputation for resourcefulness, going just to the edge and turning what you thought you knew about corporate training and consulting upside down.

Author's Note:
Cynthia Barlow

I was a healthy kid, unless you consider the hernia operation at six months of age, or the fact that I drowned three years later. Though obviously rescued and revived, I was clinically dead there for a few minutes and had a most interesting and compelling near-death experience which I was unable to articulate until many years later. That experience, I can now see, became the due north on my compass of life.

I was an athlete. Nothing special, but I played varsity field hockey, basketball and lacrosse. (Yes, I was schooled in the Middle Ages in the Mid-Atlantic.) I taught aerobics and played competitive tennis. Then a nasty nor'easter leveled me on an island and my left knee was smashed. The surgeon said when he opened it up, my knee cap was dust. Bye-bye tennis.

Two operations and extensive PT later, I can walk, and feel grateful each time I take a step.

And I can breathe, and each breath reminds me that I almost died—again—in 2005. A faulty furnace leaked carbon monoxide into my home knocking me out for four days while it fried my brain. Not quite enough to kill me, but enough to render me stupid for a few years. I bounced back from that, too. I bounced back better, primarily from implementing the concepts and practices detailed in this book.

Jennifer and I met over twenty years ago when she attended one of my leadership classes. It led her to attend The Trust Program™, and others. She brought me into the Bank of America to train her facilitators, and then into AutoZone to develop its leaders. Ours has been a consistently expanding relationship over the years. I admit to carrying a sort of maternal pride in her accomplishments. So, when she approached me about writing this book, my answer was yes. Though some of the content is based on much of what she may have absorbed from me over the years, this is *her* book; I was merely the mid-wife, and happily so.

We have both coached countless individuals and spoken to or trained countless program attendees over the course of our careers. We hear the real concerns behind the façades. Our hope is that by considering some of the ideas and information we have presented herein, you will, like us, come to believe that resilience—and the learning it engenders—is the cornerstone of successful leaders and the foundation for resilient organizations.

Resilience is not about bouncing back. It's about bouncing back *better* by building a firmer, deeper foundation for yourself and those you lead, and most especially, for those you love.

Cynthia Barlow
www.C3Conversations.com
@CynBarlow

Cynthia Barlow
Toronto, Ontario

C ynthia Barlow, President of C3 Conversations, Inc., is a facilitator, coach and team builder who specializes in creating collaborative environments through developing emotionally intelligent communication. Having conducted workshops and leadership development programs for over thirty years, her clients include top level executives to everyday people looking for ways to notch up their performance. A sample: TD Bank; Bell; Bank of America; AutoZone; Amex; CI Funds, The Ministry of Transportation, and Statistics Canada.

Through her coaching practice and intimate leadership retreats she hears the "real" truth behind the day-to-day difficulties of those who must manage others through massive change endeavors and increasingly challenging market conditions.

Cynthia's been driving new kinds of conversations for decades. These kinds of conversations build trust and propel *real* collaboration in the workplace–and at home.

A popular and experienced keynote speaker, she has inspired thousands of people to look a little deeper and reach a little higher with her direct, humorous, and slightly sassy style. She says the highest compliment she has ever received is this: "You paint word-pictures blind people can see."

Cynthia is passionate about words, water, puppies, and chocolate–which she is certain is a valid food group–and driven by truth, trust and transparency.

Bibliography & Additional Reading

Argyris, C. (2000) *Flawed Advice and the Management Trap*. New York: Oxford University Press.

Argyris, C. (1994, July-August) Good Communication That Blocks Learning. *Harvard Business Review.*

Coutu, D. (2002) How Resilience Works. *Harvard Business Review*.

Eichholz, J. C. (2017). *Adaptive Capacity*. LID Publishing.

Goffee, Robert & Jones. (September 2000) Why Should Anyone Be Led By You? *Harvard Business Review.*

Heifetz, R. & Laurie, D. (January 1997) The Work of Leadership. *Harvard Business Review.*

Heifetz, R. (1998). *Leadership Without Easy Answers*. Boston: Harvard University Press.

Heifetz, R. & Linsky, M. (2002). *Leadership on The Line*. Boston: Harvard University Press.

Heifetz, Grashow & Linsky (2009). *The Practice of Adaptive Leadership*. Boston: Harvard Business Press.

Cloud, Dr. Henry, *Integrity: The Courage to Meet the Demands of Reality*, Harper Collins, 2006.

Kegan, R. (1994) *In Over Our Heads*. Boston: Harvard University Press.

Kouzes, James M. & Barry Posner, *The Truth About Leadership*, Jossey-Bass, 2010.

Kreamer, Anne, *It's Always Personal: Emotion in the New Workplace*, Random House, 2011

Loehr, Jim & Tony Schwartz, *The Power of Full Engagement*, Simon and Schuster, 2003.

Linch, Diezemann & Dowling (2003). *The Capable Company*. Blackwell Publishing.

Mobray (2010) *Strengthening Personal Resilience*. Presentation of the Wellbeing & Performance Group.

Useem, M. (2010, November) Four Lessons In Adaptive Leadership. *Harvard Business Review.*

Acknowledgements

We wish to thank a few dedicated people who took the time to read the book in its early stages and provided meticulous, detailed feedback. Al Preble, Betsy Peck, Fran Karamousis, Gary McSherry, Ron Heifetz, Ken Bailey, Paris Aden and Halsey Cook, we are so grateful for your time and the energy. Your input made us better.

To Keith Leust for your partnership, patience and belief in us and in this project.

To Best Seller Publishing for adding sanity when we needed it most.

And to all our clients over the years—you know who you are. Thank you for teaching us. Thank you for allowing us to learn with you and from you as we grew together.

Made in USA - Kendallville, IN
83475_9781079791075
05.13.2022 1230